TABLE OF CONTENTS

Rich Wilens presents:

"Roll tide
and other stupid stuff I posted on Facebook

This book is dedicated to all professional comedians/writers who write great material. This book is all you. I am thanking you who wrote it, I am thanking you who have compiled it and I am thanking you for the finest humor I can pass along.

Sammy, Shana, Nathan, Eric, Jake
and
Eric Brian Rosenberg

ISBN-13:
978-1-942688-15-0

ISBN-10:
1-942688-15-6

Published in the United States of America

Caveat Emptor

The materials in this book: a majority of these jokes are an accumulation of ideas taken from great comedians, comedy writers, joke manuals, joke reference books, the internet, websites, Joke sites, joke blogs, tweets, public domain and people in the entertainment field.

This is done to offer you the widest selection of jokes available. for your enjoyment.

The materials were found on the internet, complied by third party web sites, who do not make any acknowledgement of the authors and consider this public domain. Authorship is given where possible and is not omitted with any malice or intent of INFRINGING on copyright ownership. Most of the jokes in this book are not original.

If any material in this book is copyrighted, infringement was not done with malice or intent to assume copyright.

Author is not held responsible for copyright infringement as the presentation of the book is a copyright of Rich Wilens and the materials are the copyright of its respective owners should they be established.

For more information for Rich Wilens to appear as a comedian in your club, public and motivational speaker, radio and television interviews, supporting actor in comedy series contact:

Rich Wilens
5505 Sioux Dr
Ocean Springs, MS 39564
(228) 238-7573
rich@Richwilens.com
Facebook: /richwilens
Skype: rich.wilens

Introduction

One of the webinars I was hosting was teaching people how to write a book. I always felt I had a book inside of me, but I wasn't sure how to bring it out. I really wasn't sure what I wanted to write about as I had so much in this small little brain of mine. So, for my first book, I elected to do a comedy book. It is a joke book and I wrote it to see if I could write a joke book.

Well it turns out I can write a joke book. So I wanted to do something different with this book and I figured out what I wanted to do. How I can present my musings.

All this stuff that I posted on Facebook is enough material to fill up a book. I found it really easy to create, procure information, put it on Facebook. I also figured out how to put it together in book form and publish it.

It's really fun to write about the things that you actually love. And I used to love telling jokes. I loved one-liners. My favorite comic was Rodney Dangerfield. Between him and George Carlin, I always wanted to be a standup comedian. But I digress…

I would scour the Internet as part of my job as an Internet marketer, wasting a lot of time, when I would come across sayings, expressions, or I would come across things, that I would express in my own words to my Facebook audience. I went ahead and posted my sayings to Facebook.

I would kick it, get stoned on some medicinal marijuana, after all I am a war hero, LOL, and things would just come out of my mouth and I would put them on Facebook.

I use Dragon NaturallySpeaking so it's really easy for me to lay back, look at something on the Internet, interpret it, put it on Microsoft Word, edit it, and presented to you. How easy is that?

Next thing I knew, I had thousands of posts that I thought it was very easy to put down in a book. Which you are reading now.

All the one-liners, jokes, sayings, are all things that have come out of my mouth that I have posted on Facebook. I guess you might say I'm addicted to Facebook.

This book is a real easy read it's basically one-liner after one-liner which equates to post after post and if you like the way I think you'll love this book.

Roll Tide

People always ask me how the hell did you come up with the title Roll Tide and other stupid stuff I posted on Facebook?

Living in Ocean Springs Mississippi, I play a lot of poker at the local casino. I'm surrounded by these Alabama nuts. These people live and breathe Alabama football.

They wear the hat, watch, tie, jacket, and when they greet each other in the hallway they scream ROLL TIDE.

I used to give all the other poker player shit when they wear the A hat, I go " what is that hat A right, Arizona right."

They would get so pissed, I bought an Alabama hat, and I would wear it and go "this is Arizona right? and watch the response.

Well of course, Alabama wins the national championship, and now you might say I'm totally on the bandwagon. Did you like them before? Hell no. But I like him now because it's a cool hat and everywhere I go people say ROLL TIDE.

I never said Roll Tide before my bar mitzvah. It's just things that Jewish boys do not say but now it just rolls off my mouth.

By the way, what's the first thing an Alabama graduate says to you when you first meet?

Would you like fries with that?

Well that just banned me from Alabama. LOL kidding

Welcome to Comedy and Rich Wilens

In 1966 in Mrs Kaminsky Math Class, I was looking out the window into the teachers parking lot of Clinton Jr. High School in Oak Park Michigan dreaming of owning the 66 red corvette convertible in the 1st spot. It belonged to Soupy Sales, a local comedian who had a kids and adult tv show. Soupy was coming to speak to us about tv, comedy and being funny.

As a kid, I used to rush home from school to have lunch or a snack with Soupy.

While everyone was learning basic math, (I can't even spell Algeabra), I was day dreaming about going into show business and I was going make a fortune as a comedian. I was the class clown. Always doing crazy stuff and cracking jokes. Be like Soupy. Yes sir. I can still do the Soupy shuffle.

Today, I was dreaming about being the next Flip Wilson, Joey Bishop, Bob Hope, Mel Brooks, Johnny Carson and George Carlin combined as the omnipotent Comedian.

I was going to buy Soupy's corvette, move to California, do movies, stand up and live the movie star life. Only problem, I was 13.

I knew I could do comedy because that dream was funny. Shit. Was it funny shit, or, shit that's funny. Funny how you can use shit in different ways. I digress.....

I knew the masters of comedy and their material as I could do George Carlin's "the 7 words you can't say on tv," Flip Wilson's

Geraldine, Victor Borge's Phonetic Language and punctuation bits, Uncle Miltie's One Liners, Johnny Carson's monologue from the night before..........but not my material. Yes, I am going somewhere with this.

I practiced and I practiced until finally I was ready. At 17? Right.

In 1971, in Carefree Arizona, I gave a stand up performance to Dick Van Dyke in his living room doing George Carlin's and Flip Wilson material. (I went to school with Stacy Van Dyke, Dicks daughter),

He said he loved it. Dick told me the delivery was great. Gave me some pointers, wished me luck, off he went and off I went. That was it?

Oh Ok, Dick. Thanks. How about getting me a gig? Nope, not going to happen. Didn't happen. Damn. "I can do tv." "I can Act too." Bye Dick ☺

I still wanted to be a comedian and I kept practicing. I would play their records, (little vinyl discs that used a needle to make sound) memorize the material and perform for whoever would listen. That's how I learned timing. Because I did not gather my own material, I was destined not to be a comedian. But I'm still funny. Sort of. Not really. No.

Fast Forward 10 years. My friends, Greg, Kyle, Bob Mead, put together a limo salesperson on a lot by telling the salesperson I was some famous comedian/actor from Arizona and we were test driving the limo..haha

I was going to perform at the world famous Comedy Store in West Hollywood. Greg said he knew somebody but we were kind of leery about that. However, he did get us a limo so I was prepared for anything.

I wasn't really sure about my material as I watched everybody perform in front of a live real comedy audience. We got there at 830 and I was hoping to go on around 10 o'clock. I enjoyed watching all the comedians get on stage, bomb, kill, work on their material, work on their timing, and doing all of this for free. I felt very comfortable and I knew I really wanted to pursue my career as a comedian.

It's getting late, about midnight but I was as ready as I would ever be and I got to go on at 2:30 in the morning.

Thanks Greg, thanks for nothing and. We were the only people left . I do have to say though it was a lot of fun and my first areas performing live in the LA comedy scene.

Even though I went on early in the morning, the experience lasted me a lifetime. Everything that I wanted to learn I learned and made a decision at this time, I am not going to be a professional comedian. Some day! But not today.

We kept the limo for a couple of days and we partied like rock stars. Back in the day we didn't know what partying like rock stars were, that's a lie, we knew what it was we just didn't take it to that extent. Thats a lie as well. We took it to an extent. I think it felt like a decade that night.

I went back to Arizona, back to work as a radio disc jockey for the local radio station and back to college to further educate myself.

Comedy was on the back burner. Gone for now but not forgotten.

Comedy in San Francisco.

I'm going to give you a little history of the comedy scene in San Francisco in 1978.

I used to do a lot of standup comedy at all the open mics in San Francisco. This was in 1977, 79, 80, etc. The comedy clubs in the city: The Other Café, The Holy City Zoo, Sam's Comedy, Cobb's Pub and the famous Punchline. I remember one night performing at the Holy City Zoo and smoking a joint with Robin Williams just outside the club chatting with him and a San Francisco cop.

That's how liberal San Francisco was back in the day. I called Robin Williams a personal friend, ask Robin do you know Rich Wilens, he goes who? Fine my perception my reality. I did meet him once.

I also appeared on comedny nights with such famous comedians. Kevin Pollock, A Whitney Brown, Dana Carvey, Harry Anderson, Marsha Warfield, and a few others.

My real friend, Frank Kidder, and his two partners: John and Anne Fox created the San Francisco comedy competition. One year at the SF comedy Competition Robin Williams came in second.

I auditioned and qualified and performed for the San Francisco comedy competition in 1978, 1979, 1980. I performed for three years.

Most of the comics didn't get paid back in the day. Most of the time we would work for food. I remember doing a comedy set at Sam's comedy, at the corner of Broadway and Kearny in North

Beach, San Francisco, for a bowl of spaghetti.

To earn that bowl of spaghetti, we used to perform for 45 minutes, and then we would go out to the front of the door at the corner of Broadway and Kearny in North Beach, San Francisco, and drag people into our comedy show.

We used to stand out and bark for people to come into the club. We used to say "live comedians here no sex here men dressed as men right here in our stage no cover charge 20 drink minimum." LOL

It was a lot of fun doing those open mics and getting all the practice performing comedy with some pretty bad material. I knew my material wasn't going to cut it in the big time, but I had a lot of fun hanging out with a bunch of these guys.

My friend, Perry Kurtz, is still doing comedy in LA. He was the MC and got me the gig at Sam's comedy.

For a real job I was working on the radio station as a radio personality for a disco station and spinning, yes a Disco DJ...One of the biggest in 1977, at one of the largest discos in San Francisco, Studio West and Eppie's at Bay and Kearny Street..

It was the biggest and largest disco in the country compared to studio 54 in New York.

Disco was in, and I became the disco God in San Francisco. Life was good in the late 70s. There was no AIDS, sex and love all around, and all the cocaine you could snort.

Actually I never liked cocaine, I just like to smell it.

From San Francisco, I moved down to the Monterey Bay area and worked at a radio station and the biggest nightclub in Monterey at the time. Early 80's Disco, Backgammon, Male Dancers, Bull Riding and comedy night..

I had a special comedy night which I emceed and I brought down some of my comedy friends, the top comics in San Francisco to perform. It was a fun time.

As time went on I had another opportunity to perform comedy. I had a client who owned a five table poker card room in Sacramento and attached to the card room was a country-western nightclub.

Not only did I get to perform with the house band, I got to play poker, and I got to have a comedy night. You talk about hitting the trifecta.

Well like all things that come to an end, my business partner died and so does the business along with enormous debt, IRS, and maybe a legal matter to that I'm sure the statute of limitations are over by now.

So now we come to the part in the book where you're saying, come on already get to the jokes. All righty then, here are the jokes. I hope you enjoy them as I enjoyed presenting them to you and as we say in Mississippi…

ROLL TIDE

(The following posts took place between January and February 2016. These events did not happen in real time)

JANUARY 2016

Girlfriend 1: Do you tell John when you've had an orgasm?
Girlfriend 2: No, he hates it when I call him at work.

She says I talk in my sleep. Funny nobody at work has ever mentioned it.

How many babies does it take to make a bottle of baby shampoo

I'm having mixed feelings about my ambivalence.

Rich: Honey, how about a quickie?
GF: As opposed to what?

Did you know Mighty Mouse is the unrecognized bastard child between Minnie Mouse and Walt Disney

Being a pessimist, I'm always right or pleasantly surprised.

Has anyone ever figured out Who put the bomp in the bomp shoo bomp shoo bomp?
Or,
Who put the dip in the dip dee dip dee dip?

GF: There a new horror film coming out called, "The Tractor!"
GF: It's pretty gruesome.
Rich: I know, I saw the trailer.

I'm so bad ass…When I go shopping,
I ALWAYS squeeze the Charmin.

2016 is off to a healthy start.........Just spent 45 minutes on the treadmill...maybe next time I'll turn it on......

If I was a sex addict, I think I would prefer group therapy.

If Super Man was gay, Do you think he would be super gay?

"Mr. Cosby, how do you plead?"
lawyer whispers in Cosby's ear
"Fleezle bop, your honor."

I'm so broke even my rain checks keep bouncing

To this day, my dog doesn't know she was adopted.

Two of my girlfriend's favorite toys are called Buzz and Woody

You win some You lose some if you're lucky, you get some

Bumper Sticker: My drop-out son makes $100,000 a year selling Pot to your Honor student

She was truly stunning. Especially after she tased me.

If you are ever attacked by a gang of angry clowns... Protect yourself and always go for the juggler.

Pet insurance will not pay for medicinal marijuana to my dog. I call bullshit!

Just saw a license plate that said J3WBACA...oy

How long do I have to lay on my couch in the same position before I can call it yoga?

My Body Mass Index can only be calculated with pi.

My bookkeeper is crazy. She says she keeps hearing invoices.

Is there nothing like a multiple-choice rhetorical question?
A: Yes
B: No
C: Maybe
D: Does not require a response
E: Um, D was a response

How to give a TED talk:
1) Find someone named Ted.
2) Make him talk.

If you say, Introducing Mr and Mrs Bruce and Caitlyn Jenner...
you will confuse people..
but technically you won't be wrong...

There are 47 people named "Lol" in the U.S. Their parents names are usually OMG and WTF
If you tell the airport you lost your son, Kevin McCallister, they have to announce it on the loudspeaker,
and it brightens everyone's day

If Darth Vader had bothered to wear a condom, he'd be ruling the universe right now.

GF: Do you think the world will ever end?
Rich: I don't think so, its round.

"Use the fork, Luke." - Obi-Wan Kenobi teaching table manners.

"Follow me on Vine!" - Tarzan.

Let's put "fun" back in "dysfunctional."

I'd rather jingle only part of the way.

Whenever there's a meeting of the Premature Ejaculators Club everyone comes early.

A gay porn star named Rock Bottom.

Bear with me, I have a bear with me.

This coffee is so strong it could be my password

Just noticed that the movie where Rocky lost, was called Rocky One.

I officially weigh more than my bank account balance

You know you're having a bad month when Sheldon Cooper is having more sex than you.

I've heard the phrase "He's a complete idiot..."
Has anyone ever heard of an incomplete one?

I'm learning to cobble, it will be good for my sole.

Do you think if you're pregnant and use a vibrator, there is a chance your child will be born with a stutter?

Did you know the international symbol for marriage is a white flag?

My body is not my temple, It's like a sports bar & grill.

I call my internet girlfriend "e-bae."

The one flight attendant on my American Airlines plane was so old I overheard her talking about her threesome
with the Wright brothers.

I can hit the side of a barn..

But what if you're addicted to cold turkey?

I'm on this raw food diet where I eat my Chef Boyardee
out of the can without heating it up.
.

Is dreaming of a white Christmas racist

I would really like to go bowling, but I don't have time to spare.

I have a talking scale, I don't know how much I weigh, because every time I go to stand on it.....it cries...Cries one person at a time…

I've decided, I'm going back to traffic school to get my Masters.

I just read a news headline that Jared Fogle is appealing.. I wonder if that's a quote from his cell mate

I enjoyed the Japanese trailer of the new Star Wars film. I'm not happy they've renamed it "Super Happy Awesome Space Robot Laser Movie"

It was a true Hanukkah miracle for me this year. My hash oil lasted 8 nights.

I decided my Jedi name will be, Oddly-Long-Kajones

Thomas Jefferson died in enormous debt. You know what I call that? Winning.

I saw mommy swipe right on Santa Claus.

Bored while sitting in the parking lot? Put a sticky notes on people's cars saying "sorry for the damage. Then watch them. Priceless.

There's nothing worse than a knowledgeable idiot.

I thought alcoholic anonymous meetings was a place to go get drunk in secret.

Dad: What's that pile of dirty clothes doing on the bathroom floor?
Jake: It's a dead Jedi, Dad.

I may be alone on this but I really like playing Solitaire by myself

I called Erik instead of Eric and he didn't even notice.

Gambling addiction helplines would be so much more effective if every 10th caller was a winner.

If you don't want your children to be spoiled, store them in the refrigerator.

No matter how old you are, during Christmas, an empty wrapping paper tube is still a light saber.

If you plan to fail then it's ok if you failed because you succeeded in failing and that makes you a winner!

Going to put TSAPre✔ in my bio.

If you look up the word "dictionary" in a dictionary the definition should say, "Really?"

If you surround yourself with negative people, negative things will happen. If you surround yourself with positive people you should get tested

The DMV asked me if I wanted to be an organ donor but I told them I only owned a piano.

Decided to start a sex toy drive for those in need this holiday season.

Jake: Dad, tell me again how when you were my age you had to walk all the way across the living room to change the channel.

No matter how hard you try, you cannot baptize a cat.

My new bank manager name is Gilbert O'Sullivan. I went to see him the other day. A loan again, naturally.

That moment in the night when you're peeing in the dark and the noise of water hitting the toilet bowl stops. But you're still peeing.

If you owe everything you have to your wife... You should have hired a better lawyer

GF: Stop patronizing me!
Rich: Do you even know what that means?

Godfather pizza is a terrible name for a mafia front business

1500 Pepsi workers have been giving their pink slips today... They all tested positive for Coke.

Woman: I think I'm a nymphomaniac.
Psychiatrist: I can help you. but my fee is $120 an hour.
Woman: How much for the entire evening?

My girlfriend and I have been together long enough that "Netflix and Chill" actually means Netflix and chill.

MISSED CONNECTION: I was the Keymaster, you were Zuul.

The bad news for Jared is that his wife divorced him. The good news is that he's the penitentiary's most eligible bachelor.

'Tis the season to forget how to spell "it's"

Who doesn't get that great sense of pleasure when your fart causes someone to open a car window?

Believe It Or Not: Chef Bobby Flay is married to Sue Flay. :)

If you have oral sex with an anorexic woman is it called skinny dipping?

If you soak Van Halen's Lead singer in hot water you get David Lee Broth.

Naysayers rarely use the word nay.

Nothing good ever follows the phrase "This is going to hurt a little"

A pair of cows were talking in the field.
One says, "Have you heard about the mad cow disease that's going around?"
"Yeah." The other cow says,
"Makes me glad I'm a penguin."

"You know that look women get when they want sex? Me neither."

Two hunters are out in the woods when one of them collapses. He's not breathing and his eyes are glazed. The other guy whips out his cell phone and calls 911.
I think my friend is dead! he yells. What can I do?
The operator says, Calm down. First, let's make sure he's dead.
There's a silence, then a shot. Back on the phone, the guy says,
Okay, now what?

It's Sunday. Let's go take pictures of brunch.

"Sometimes you win, sometimes you learn."

Opening my eyes has really opened my eyes to a lot of things.

Living in the past is great except the commute to work takes forever

"My girlfriend makes me want to be a better person - so I can get a better girlfriend."

Sloths are my business and business is very slow.

The only one true connection is the Andrea & to that I say thrice more * I know: 1977 wants it joke back *

Quitters never prosper unless they are the greatest quitters of all

I tried to MSG you but I am out of monosodium glutamate

What came first: clothes or clothesline?

(The following posts took place between December and January 2015. These events did not happen in real time)

December 2016

On Black Friday I woke up at 4am to save $10.
I then used that $10 to buy myself breakfast which
I wouldn't have needed had I been sleeping.
"I don't fail, I succeed at finding what doesn't work."
My GF put so many words in my mouth, I wound up having a vowel movement.

I keep my dreams alive.. by hitting the snooze button.

I'm a stud muffin, are you my cupcake? :)

So Black Friday isn't a hip new Dragnet reboot?

There's always so much sexual tension in the workplace when I work from home.

I have good news and bad. Bad News: I have insomnia.
Good News: I won't die in my sleep.

You should not live your life comparing yourself to others. But talking to a total loser once in a while will make you feel better.

It's Thanksgiving eve. Don't forget to set the scales back ten pounds...

How come they're called screwdrivers and not screwscrewers

"Take my wives, please!" - Mormon Brigham Youngman.

nurse flips on light switch The doctor will see you now.

I'm a folder. So all toilet paper is eight ply for me.

Ben Carson just said: "Thomas Jefferson ran a dry cleaning business and was married to a woman named Weezy."

My Holiday Checklist: 1. Buy clay 2. Make dreidels 3. Wait for them to be dry and ready 4. Play dreidel. Duh.

Working on my next book: The 7 Habits of High and Effective People

At this years Marketing Mayhem I'd like to see Poison open for The Cure . That would be sick.

It's not fair to call Muslim terrorists; "Muslim terrorists" even though Muslim terrorists call themselves Muslim terrorists?

My son Jake's new career plan is to hope that someone who looks like him gets famous so he can become an impersonator.

It's been so long since I had sex, I need a city permit to get an erection.

I bought a $200.00 dollar tent so I can camp outside Best Buy for 3 days and save $10.00 on a TV.

Wouldn't it be cool if they could design microwave popcorn to pop all at once?

Aim high, shoot high, do everything high.

Im apathetic and I don't care who knows it.

Darth Vader: Luke, I am your father. Luke Skywalker: I'm a vegan.

Lois Lane: Clark, why don't your eyeglasses have prescription lenses?
Clark Kent: I'm a hipster, Lois.

Nobody wished me a happy birthday today, which is good because today's not my birthday.

Who called them donuts and bagels and not hole foods

The popcorn button on the microwave should turn any food into popcorn.

One man's rock bottom is another man's rock bottom.

Give a man a fish and he'll eat for a day. Teach a man to fish and you'll have a cold-blooded fish killer on your hands.

I took a shower today and now I'm not allowed in Home Depot anymore.

Maybe I don't want to have a nice day, okay? You can't tell me what to do…

I'm not a procrastinator because I don't get paid to crastinate.

I went to Olive Garden because I want to feel like I'm with family but not actually be with my family.

Donald Trump says he would bring back waterboarding, but he'd make it classier by using Perrier.

I hope Brussels is doing everything in their power to protect their delicious sprouts.

"Money talks, bullshit walks." - inventor of talking money and walking bullshit.
I've eaten bacon today. Please pray for me.

"Head, shoulders, knees and toes, knees and toes." - young cannibal ordering dinner.

There's only one ward at Peek-A-Boo Hospital. The I.C.U.

Can't help but to wonder if Flavor Flav set his clock back.

Still no cure for being sick of it all.

Ben Carson is what happens when neurosurgeons are allowed to operate on themselves.

how many babies does it take to make a bottle of baby shampoo?

Before the internet was invented it was really hard to Google things.

I added insult to injury and got iinnsjuulrty.

I thought the illuminati was an Italian brothers' light fixture business.
Jared Fogle was happy with his 15 year sentence.
He was hoping for anything under 18 years

Marijuana is now legal in Washington D.C.
I bet it was some Joint Legislative Committee.

Casper may be a 'friendly' ghost but he still must atone for his earthly digressions, immoralities & sins before being allowed to ascend

You know you're out of shape when you nearly pass out from getting something out of the bottom drawer of the fridge

I used to think the best part of waking up was Folgers in my cup, until I replaced Folgers with whiskey in my cup.

It's so weird. I have insomnia all day then when night hits, I'm fast asleep.

If you walk more than 15 feet away from your cart in the grocery store I will freeking hide it from you. Lol

My life is so exciting I just naturally assume there is a fly on the wall sharing the moment with me

We should also screen that immigrant from the North Pole with the beard who wears funny suits that puts unidentified packages in our houses.

Why are we bringing into this country 10,000 Syrian refugees when we have homeless veterans on the street?

Mistress: Wow! Darling this is great.
Whore: Come on! Finish it now.
Girlfriend: Ah! Please slowly.
Wife: Ceiling needs painting!

I'm a seaweed enthusiast. —I see weed, I smoke it. lol I know...sorry

In the land of the blind the one eyed man drives

GF: All men are the same.
Rich: Who told you to try them all?

They say once you go black you never go back. Well once you go Jewish, I can get you a discount.

So do you think Charlie Sheen wishes he had a magic johnson?

Another year goes by where I am not named People's Sexiest Man of the year. I just don't understand. #Bullshit

ISIS's online 24-hour help desk: "Hi my vest won't explode." "Is it plugged in?" "Of course! Oh. I'm such an idi..."

The person who cuts my hair used to be a dog groomer. She never lets me leave without tying a bandana around my neck.

Every time you use the word "refugee" a royalty fee is paid to Tom Petty & the Heartbreakers.

Is there a non-creepy way to tell a woman, "I love the half naked pictures you post on-line and would love to see more?" I'm asking for a friend.

Why do religious people have a problem with same sex marriages? Since when did marriage involve sex?

New Orleans is playing Oklahoma City. So it's NO vs OK.

Charlie Sheen has changed his status on Facebook to " It's Positive ".

Rich: Honey, nothing is better than you.
GF: Oooh how love - - - wait a minute, what?

I forgot to promote my book, "7 habits of highly forgetful people."

When I was 12 I found a dominatrix porn mag.
I took it home and put it under my bed. My parents found it,
but they never spanked me again. Damn :)

I sold my guitar to a guy with no arms recently.
I asked him how it was going to work, he replied,
'I'm going to play it by ear'."

I had an argument with one of the seven dwarfs. He wasn't happy.

Watson! I've overdosed on Immodium!" "No shit, Sherlock

54% of Americans now support the legalization of marijuana. Those
figures seem a little "high" to me.

Has enough time passed that it's OK to admit I purchased the Vanilla
Ice album To The Extreme?

Winnie the Pooh and I have the same eating habits.
I love honey, I use my hands, and when I eat I don't wear pants.

How do you apply for anti-social security?

If I can't hear, see, taste, smell, or touch you... Then we really have no common sense. Goodnight Gracie

Can only imagine what kind of stats Drew Brees
could put up if he could play against his own defense

If you take earthworms to Mars, do you have to change their name?

If you can't handle me at my worst, then you sure as hell don't deserve to call yourself an existential psychotherapist.

I'm not too old to "Netflix and Chill" I am however too old to SAY "Netflix and Chill," apparently..
I'm so sick of waitin' for the tally man to tally my bananas...

Lesbian MILFS. The world's greatest oxymoron.

They say you'll never get over your fears unless you conquer it. When I was a kid, I was afraid of heights. Now, I'm high all the time.

I ate a bowl of cherries & was not once reminded of life

Holm/Rousey: I haven't seen an upset like that since Daniel LaRusso beat Johnny Lawrence in the All-Valley Karate Championship.

I'm spending today at the beaches burying junk metal items with a note: 'Get a life!' written on them.

I've just got a job at an erectile dysfunction clinic. It not a hard job to do.

Judge in Utah ruled that a lesbian couple's adopted child would be better of with a traditional family, like a man and his six sister wives.

I've become so lazy I can't be bothered ' procrasturbating'.

If your bad at oral sex, that would qualify as having an eating disorder.

Lionel Richie: Hello. Is it me you're looking for? Starbucks barista: Yes. Your drink is ready.

My dream? To have sex on Pluto. Unfortunately, all my relationships are strictly PLUTONIC

I bring a rabbit's foot to the casino for luck. Today I saw a woman with a camel toe. I don't know how she got that thing on a keychain.

I like to pee while I'm drinking a bottle of water. The sight blows my dog's mind.

How much different would the world be if Alice Cooper played the accordion?

It's so weird being over 50-years-old, I enjoy looking at kitchen appliances as much as I enjoy looking at the boobs of 18-year-old college girls.

Rich, describe your normal morning: Well, I start off with a puppy video and then slowly find out what people are mad about So Facebook? Yea

As a Jew I have strict dietary restrictions, so I'm not allowed to eat at expensive restaurants.

You've never realized how weird your friends are until you describe them to someone else.

Religion is considered to be true by the common, false by the wise and useful by the rulers.

I tried to reinvent myself but then I realized I never invented myself

The first mistake a lot of pirates make is burying their treasure on a place called Treasure Island. It's sort of a giveaway.

(The following posts took place between November and December 2015. These events did not happen in real time)

NOVEMBER 2015

It just occurred to me....."Jiffy Lube" would be my gay porn name....

It's not fair to judge people by their looks... Especially the ugly ones.

**When someone tells me "Thank you for your service,
I politely say it's not necessary.
The privilege is mine to serve my country which I did.
For that, Thank you for letting me serve you.**~ Rich Wilens

I ordered the Meatlovers Supreme sushi roll.

My final request for when I die and get cremated is to fill my pockets with corn kernels.

I imagine being a yo-yo salesman has its ups and downs.

Starbucks doesn't have any army men on their holiday cups, they must hate Veterans.

Rich: Tell me a quality about yourself
GF: I'm a great listener
Rich: anything else?
GF: *looks up from phone* what?

The Terminally ill Star Wars fan dies one week after special screening of The Force Awakens. His last words: "I'm dying just like Chewie!"

Starbucks took off reindeers. Last time I checked reindeers are with Santa Claus, not with Jesus

People say Jesus used to be a Carpenter… I got all their records. He doesn't sing on any of them.

I guess Finding Dory is not as a horrific sequel title as Frying Nemo.

A homeless guy at the light just told me to smile. There is probably a lesson here but he needs to mind his own fucking business.

Is your clown posse insane? The answer may surprise you!

Where all the Jews? What I really want to see is an Hasidic zombie...that would be amazing Walking Dead episode

Starbucks is said to hate Christmas so much that all of its eggnog will be made from Egg Beaters..

Whoever wrote "Twinkle, Twinkle Little Star" obviously never studied astronomy.

Did you know that Jesus was a practicing Jewish rabbi? His Starbucks cup would definitely have Happy Hannukah on it

Thank God Starbucks changed their holiday cups. We were running perilously low on fabricated controversies

Told the Starbucks barista my name was Jesus to protest War on Christmas and he insisted on pronouncing it Jesús. They are Satan's children.

I woke up this morning feeling like exercising. ".
Thank G-d I went back to sleep till that feeling passed

GF: If you want to break up with me do it while I'm eating kale because chances are your breakup is the second worst thing happening to me

Every year James Bond stands in line at the DMV for two hours renewing his license to kill.

I met the jewish 007. His real name is baum - Wein-baum

Anything less sincere that a the cop who pulled you over saying "Have a nice day"?

My GF says I am truly multi-talented. I can talk and piss her off at the same time.

Rich: Siri, When will the world end? Siri: If I knew, I'd tell you so you could bring me to life for a day. We will get ice-cream and run on the beach.

My eyes are tearing and my nose is stuffy watching the new Charlie Brown movie . Looks like I'm allergic to Peanuts.

Don't trust any doctor who tells you to put the lime in the coconut and drink them both together.

Being the cheap guy at the strip club is the most alone you'll ever feel. A good setting for deep thought.

My Alaskan geography is horrible. I really need to get my Berings Strait.

I'm so tired by the end of it, I often think it should be renamed weakend.

I hate it when people flip me off while I'm driving. On the other hand, I love it when I flip people off while I'm driving.

Waking up with an uncharged phone feels like you wasted a whole night of sleep.

My problem is, people telling me what my problem is.

Are you an introvert if you tell people?

Gotta be ironic when u get in a wreck while driving a Focus

There are only 2 words in life that will open a lot of doors for you... Push and Pull.

There is a new StarTrek show coming to CBS. It's CBS, so the show's name will be 'NCIS: Outer Space.'

Some days you're the flying squirrel and some days you're the moose.

I'm the least gullible person in the world... So I've been told.

I just put some vegetable flavored seasoning on my vegetables, Not stoned...

If you can't get an automatic faucet to turn on, you have just achieved a new low self esteem.

My neighborhood is so tough if you were the first to say, shotgun before getting in the car, you got to ride holding the shotgun.

Better to be lucky than good or lucky and good?

Daylight Savings Time is quite a setback for me

Halloween is the hardest day of the year to talk extremist Muslims out of their belief that America is just an evil country full of whores.

If Boy George really slept with Prince, then he should be known as "The Purple Peter Eater."

My Halloween Poem: Pumpkins are orange and candy is yummy You better give me treats or at least some freeking money

When someone is sad I tell them it could be worse, they could be a be Alabama fan

"You jerkoff!" Is my favorite insult that's also a command.

I'm revising my prediction: Mets in 12

I'm currently on a cleanse. It wasn't intentional, but now, thanks to last night's Taco Bell, I'm on one.

Now hiring ghostwriters for my Twitter feed. Must have 5+ years experience being mediocre

Uncle Ben has been working with converted rice for so long,he admits that he is now Ben Gay.

Sex is a euphemism for sex.

So I'm watching Its The Great Pumpkin Charlie Brown and it dawns on me.....Lucy is a bitch

Why is a cake the only food we write on? When I order a sandwich from Subway & they ask what I want on it, I say, 'Happy Birthday, Rich !'

When having Kinky sex.........never choose "More" as a safe-word

On my tombstone I want the words, "What the hell was that all about?"

One thing you can say about stoners, they always take the high road.

Al Bundy is my spirit animal

If I compliment you, I mean it. If I sound sarcastic, it's because I hate that I mean it.

I'm too lazy to carve a Jack O' Lantern this Halloween. Instead I'm just gonna draw a scary face on a pumpkin spice latte from Starbucks..

No matter how many times I listen to it, the song "forever young" never gets old.

I am a hobbyist of sorts. I collect coins from all the great fountains of the world

I blame everyone for my inability to blame myself.

Sing Sing prison was one Sing away from being a song by Louis Prima. I could have busted out of a Prima song. (too old for you guys, huh?)

They say that Santa is always watching. Well if he was watching 10 minutes ago, he's a total perv!
I left instructions after my death to ignore all previous instructions.

Just watched an hour of online porn to check out the latest tattoo trends.

I don't understand it. I have a house, a car, a job and good credit. My mother would tell you I am a catch. And yet, my steak and my sex life are the same: very rare...

every seven in one people have multiple personalities

Man leaves heart in San Francisco, UPS unable to find owner.

I now go to the 99 Cent Only Store with confidence. Thats the true sign of resignation.

You might say I'm a "Prograsstinator" [pro-grass-te-ne-tar] person who puts off projects and responsibilities due to (alleged) use of pot.

Some days I wake up ready to put on my Cape & Cowl to fight crime. Most days I end up wearing my hooded snuggie and play in my blanket fort

The thing about women's rights is that women are always right.

[at vet] Rich: hows my dog
Vet: we had to put him down [gets interrupted]
Rich: WHAT!
Vet:... from the table as he wouldn't sit still.. Vet humor (idiots)

Terry Crews and his wife completed a 90-Day 'Sex Fast'. Sex fast? If I had sex once in 90 days I considered that a good three months.

Just got back from Scarborough fair? Forgot half the things I went for. Got the parsley and sage, but no rosemary and thyme. Damn!

You don't really meet that many jive turkeys these days

Just like Hendrix I always pardon myself before kissing the sky

A man has been sentenced to five years in prison for using counterfeit chips at a poker tournament in an Atlantic City casino after he attempted to flush $2.7 million worth of them down the toilet of his hotel room. The question is, is dumping a bunch of poker chips down the toilet considered a "royal flush" or a "straight flush?"

How about a Latin-American zombie named Joaquin Dead.

I didn't choose the Twitter life, the Twitter life chose me.

This is my My Tinder Bio: I'm just a donkey looking for my Shrek.

Lamar Odom regained consciousness, opened his eyes, saw Kim and said HI !... She says, STILL?

I think it's cute Canada had elections too. It's almost like they're a real country.

The easiest way to become a millionaire, is to start out as a billionaire.

Life is like a box of chocolates. You're always left with the one no one else wanted.

My life coach just cut me from the team.

If you nail a tool shed closed, how do you put the hammer away
Just because your penis implant didn't go well, you don't have to go off half cocked...

I hate going to a children's zoo. I always wonder how their parents can allow them to be kept in those tiny cages.

I find it depressing to take antidepressants

I thought my vasectomy would stop my wife from getting pregnant but it just changed the color of the baby instead

How to Lose a Guy in 10 Sec "I know it's only our 2nd date, but... I think I'm in love w you." This has been: How to Lose a Guy in 10 Sec

Remember...you matter to someone...that person probably doesn't matter but still

I get why you don't tug on superman's cape spit into the wind or pull the mask off ol'lone ranger but what's this about jim??

My Hallmark Card: I think I would get you / If you were a disease.

How to piss off a pregnant woman....... Just be around and breathe.

Spiderman wouldn't be much help in the middle of the desert

I went vegan for a few hours didnt take but I still feel nice and superior

Do you know what just dawned on me? The age of aquarius

T-Shirt alert. Old bowlers never die. They just end up in the gutter

The ear infection I have is from listening to my girl friend talk dirty to me.

(The following posts took place between November and December 2015. These events did not happen in real time)

October 2015

My GF said she is depressed and unhappy. Ugh... I hate morning people

Missed connection: I asked you over to help with my wifi. You helped fix my wifi
My GF thinks Lenny Kravitz is so hot. She told me, "You know what they say: The blacker the berry, the sweeter the Jews."

I'd really like to be a film set designer, but I don't want to make a scene.

I'm hungry. My GF said make yourself a sandwich. If I could make myself a sandwich, I wouldn't make myself a sandwhich. I would make myself an 21 year old billionaire

Q: "Senator Clinton, how will your presidency not be a third term of President Obama?" Hillary: "I don't have a penis"

If you have sex with your clone, is it incest, gay or masturbation?

It doesn't matter who's the Sexiest Woman Alive , any guy would still have sex with the woman who ranked 1,000,001 on the list.

This years Halloween costume: I'm going as an able-bodied man who gets a monthly disability check.

If I ever die from excessive masturbation, I want my cause of death to be listed as "Multiple Strokes".
In honor of National Coming out day we should focus on the next step. What to do after? I suggest binge watch Queer as Folk, Will and Grace or Golden Girls.

Don't attempt a Mentos / Diet Coke enema! Never mind how I know.

I think the Ground Hog be the symbol of National Coming Out Day ...if he see's his shadow.....you are gay for 6 more years.

God, if you want me to go into outdoor advertising, just give me a sign.

Dont tell me when to hold 'em, fold 'em, walk away or run, bitch

Here in Mississippi a great friend is someone who will drive home drunk for you since you already have 4 DUIs and they only have 2

"You hide your weight well" is the most odd compliment. It's people saying you're fat, but that your fat is really good at hide and seek

"The mai tai got its name when two Polynesian alcoholics got in a fight over some neckwear."

"I don't have to tell you it goes without saying there are some things better left unsaid. I think that speaks for itself. The less said about it the better."

I got a job offer to become a fitness model. I do all the 'before' shots.

I have a topiary hedge fund.

Old mechanics never die. They just lose their motor skills.

It's great that a Campbell's soup ad featured two gay dads, but it'd be even better if the ad featured two lesbian moms for clam chowder.

Let's just say that people will think twice about using that bathroom from now on.

If you think your cat needs a new scratching post, you obviously have enough time to build it yourself

The glass is never half full or half empty when you lower expectations

God: I 'm going to make an animal that's attracted to light but it only appears at night. I'll name it 'moth' oy

All I'm saying is that when God was making animals, Guinea Pigs may have been the first try at making a Pig.

Jake: can I ask a question?
Dad: sure Jake: how do you spell 'Simone'?
Dad: like Simon, but with an e
Jake: *writes* Semone

"Former British Bands for $300, Alex." -This band's name sounds like your colon after eating White Castle.

"What is Chumbawumba?"

Some people like to experiment sexually. I'm the control group.

I need to learn how to be patient.... NOW!

The hardest part of procrastinating is discovering you're actually depressed.

Q. Which Empire did Dick Van Dyke stumble over?
A. The Ottoman

It's never a good sign if you hear her sigh half way through sex It's probably not good if she looks at her watch either Or starts reading

Old rock stars never die. They just begin to fret more.

35% of people 65 and older use social networking sites. In case you were wondering where all the hot GILFs on Facebook were coming from.

My New Invention is a toilet seat with a built in scale so you can weigh yourself before and after.

First Al Roker and now John Goodman? Where have all my fat role models gone?

I didn't choose the thug life. The thug life was chosen for me by a career assessment quiz.

I got tired of ironing my shirts so I injected them with botox

Hoping tomorrow I get the call and I finally win the Nobel Peace Prize. I've been overlooked for years. Enough with the bullshit.

There is no prison that can hold me. Not the way I want to be held.

When I grow up I want to be an ancient astronaut theorist.

I wish I could go back in time and make the same mistakes all over again

I've already hit my 4 hours work for the week. I could take a 5 day weekend. Or I could whore myself out for more cash. Probably whore.

I don't have to disagree with you to think you're an idiot!

If you watch a Pink Floyd DVD on Blue Ray, does it come out Deep Purple?

National Dyslexia Day is celebrated on both 9-6 and 6-9.

I'm following my dreams back to bed.

GF: "Don't the flowers make the garden look beautiful."
Rich: "No. People make the garden look beautiful."
GF: "Okay. Seriously. Stop."

Do you know the meaning of the word "sycophant"? Please, I'll totally kiss your ass if you tell me.

If you are lucky enough in this life to have one really good friend, you can provide an alibi for just about anything.

I finally got my bike out of the shop and I joined a motorcycle gang. You've heard of Dykes on Bikes? I joined Dudes on Ludes

I'm starting a handicapped prostitution ring called "Feels on Wheels."

You can tell a lot about a person by asking "Pinkerton or Blue Album?," especially if they answer, "What?"
Porn company employees accused of "inside-her trading"

Before alleys were invented alley cats had nowhere to go.

The sailors say rando, you're a fine girl, what a good wife you would be.

"Don't You (Forget About Me)" is one of my favorite songs from that band whose name I can't remember.

Sometimes I don't even want to smoke a little medicinal pot but I'm home alone so I have to.

Now that they found water on Mars, how long before they bottle it & sell it at Whole Foods for $19?

I assume the hardest part of being in a street gang is not being able to enjoy a Frappuccino in public.

Just took an Entourage character quiz online and got herpes.

Nothing makes a joke feel more dumb than having to explain it to a stranger over the Internet.
See Spot. See Spot run. See Spot fall. See Spot injure C6 and C7.
Spot sees spots.

Maybe it is time for Chef Boyardee to become Chef Manardee

I'm just trying to monetize my laziness

If it weren't for spam, nobody would call me "my dear"

The Vatican fires a gay Priest. Why? Because the one thing the Church that professes love for your fellow man hates most is love for your fellow man.

My idea of an all-niter is not getting up to go pee...

When the going gets tough, I go to the bathroom.

Take control of your destiny. Shop naked at Walmart.

Taco Sunday, Taco Monday, and Taco Tuesday. You can add taco to any day and make it better

Chocolate - the gift that says 'I didn't care enough to put any effort into getting you something'

About to see an 80s cover band. I hope the experience brings me back to the good ole days when I was 8.

I know I'm not supposed to take a donkey down this road, but don't blame me because it's the asphalt.

Yesterday wanted to change the world. Today I want to change myself. Tomorrow I will need someone to do that for me.

Im apathetic and I don't care who knows it.

I called my friend Geoff instead of Jeff and he didn't even notice. OK I'll stop

I called my friend Sean instead of Shawn and he didn't even notice.

I called my friend Meaghan instead of Megan and she didn't even notice.

Saw 'The Martian' today. It's amazing how much more sophisticated the special effects have gotten since 'The Moon Landing' in 1969.

Pre-Natal Prozac Solving problems before they arise.

I'll never understand those who step outside because they need some fresh air, then light up a smoke while inhaling said fresh air.

"Hey Rich, how's it going?"
"Awful, I just want to forget about everything right now"
"Oh I'm sorry. What's wrong?"
"I don't know, I forgot"

I got offered a permanent position at work whilst working from home and not wearing pants.

The real walk of shame is returning from the buffet table with only a plateful of salad.

Caitlyn Jenner should dress up as Bruce for Halloween just to confuse the shit out of everybody.

To be safe, keep all your money hidden in your mattress. And then keep your mattress in a money market account.

I like to name my cats after hurricanes. Cat 1,Cat 2,Cat 3,Cat 4,Cat 5

Why did the Italian baker make spectacles out of bread? To Ciabatta!

Everything I have ever learned I learned from a poster titled

Everything I ever learned I learned from a poster.

I'm not sure if that's a fig tree in my backyard, or just a figment of my imagination.

It's World Vegetarian Day so today so grab a McRib....and stare at people eating salads...........

Diet Root Beer was created so people who show up late for picnics will have something to drink.

I found two Black Eyed Peas,in a Podcast.

Thinking of dressing up as a blessing in disguise for Halloween.
(The following posts took place between October and November 2015. These events did not happen in real time)

I'm like a newspaper; nobody reads me anymore.

It concerns me when someone comes out of the bathroom stall and has to wash their hands all the way up to their elbows

The only thing worse than being stuck at a party where you don't know anyone is being stuck at one where you do.

There is nothing common about my sense

You need a Snickers when you eat too much kale and you need a reason to stop crying
In Alabama growing a beard is classified as a full time job.

Whole Foods Market plans to cut 1,500 jobs over the next 8 weeks and pass on the savings directly to themselves.

Does anyone smell pizza or am I having the best stroke ever?

Of course, Tony the Tiger loves Frosted Flakes. If that is all you feed him

It's not even October 1. Anyone but me already tired of Pumpkin?

I look at buffets the same way I look at masturbating. The greatest amount of pleasure followed by the greatest amount of shame
No son, when i was your age i didn't have to walk barefoot to school in the snow but i did have to use dial up internet.

(The following posts took place between November and December 2015. These events did not happen in real time)

September 2015

Thinking about getting a semicolon tattoo to show my support for punctuation marks.

I always felt sorry for the pedophiles on "To Catch a Predator" because they never got to finish their lemonade and cookies.

Correct me if im wrong but is it wrong to correct you?

how do they make those collars small enough to fit on a flea
How did Spock protect himself from STDs? He wore vulcanized rubbers.

Today is the day after Yom Kippur....or as Chinese Restaurants call it....BLACK THURSDAY!

I'm writing a horror movie about werewolf nuns called "Creature of Habit."

Relationship goals: I would much rather have a blind date, than with a deaf banana

You've got to hand it to nerds, because they can't catch.

Unlike Rick Astley, I will give you up.

My ex wife was feared by all my neighbors because they believe she practiced black magic and was responsible for missing cats and dogs and strange sounds at all hours. Every time we fought, my wife would scream and yell always threating me the same statement: "When I die I will dig my way up and out of the grave to come back and haunt you for the rest of your life!"

Well she died abruptly under strange circumstances and the funeral I had a closed casket. After the burial, I went straight to the local bar and began to party as if there was no tomorrow. The cheerfulness of my actions was becoming extreme while the neighbors approached in a group to ask these questions: Are you not afraid? Worried? Concerned?

She practiced black magic and stated when she died she would dig her way up and out of the grave to come back and haunt you for the rest of your life?
"Let the bitch dig. I had her buried upside down."

Kermit parks in Handicapped Frog space and gets toad.

Study finds that it is safe for heart attack survivors to have sex. No word on whether sex is safe for those that didn't survive.

If you neglect to send a Get Well card & the person dies is it appropriate to send an Oh Well card?

Wearing your team's jersey while watching football is like getting naked to watch porn.

Watson: "What kind of information does the Periodic Table hold??"
Sherlock: "Elementary, my dear Watson."

If it had been called "Yum Kippur", then you would be able to eat something.
Yom Kippur is the only time of the year l witness Jews starving.

Today is Yom Kippur (aka the day of atonement where we are forgiven for not calling our mothers enough).

Ben Carson was asked if an agnostic can be president. ...he said he's not sure...

Today is Yom Kippur, the Jewish day of atonement. This is the day Jews around the world ask for forgiveness for Adam Sandler

The difference between North & South Korea is that South Korea has a Seoul.

{Speed date} Her: It says here on your bio you're a lawyer
Him: Actually, I'm a pathological liar
Her: close enough

Nothing worse than a fool with a valid point

In high school I was given the title "Most Original", which is probably the nice way of saying "The Weirdest"

I'm opening an Atoning Salon. One day only..Fast service for Yom Kippur

Have anyone seen a cow laugh so hard, milk come out her nose?

I had to explain to my GF that Tupac Shakur is not a Jewish holiday.

Temptation should never be mistaken for opportunity.

"Your Mama is So Ugly Hello Kitty Says Goodbye to Her

I'm ready to write a Christian based romantic book series called Loveiticus

They say your kids grow up and move out in the blink of an eye. I'm blinking like a madman and Jake's still here.

"Gosh I hate seeing Alabama lose," said no one outside Tuscaloosa. George Zimmer from Mens Wearhouse says he has been smoking pot for 50 years. I would buy from him his private stash. He would guarantee it and you would like the way you feel.

Rule Tide in Tuscaloosa, Alabama tonight says Ole Miss.......

Tonight I'm gonna party like I have $19.99.

When you look like you're trying to puncture a juice box with an earthworm, you might want to try Viagra…

"The Who postponed their tour."
"Who?"
"Yes."
"Yes postponed their tour?"
"No, The Who."
"Who?"
"Yes."
"Yes postponed their tour?"

I value my privacy, but if logging in with FB means I don't have to register then yes have all my info.

I'm genuinely excited that iOS9 has slightly different font so the answer is no I don't have any friends
Money isn't everything, but it sure keeps my kids in touch.

If you want to see a grown man cry and be happy at the same time... Have his ex-wife go off a cliff in his brand new Porsche.

Do girls named Destiny ever worry about their future?

If you want to quit hair school half way through a lesson, do you just get up and weave.

Went to a Sex Addicts anonymous meeting the other day. What a bunch of jerk offs.
If Steve Jobs gets 2 movies, Zig Ziglar should get at least 1, right? I mean, if we're going to make movies about marketers....

Teenager Ahmed Mohamed was arrested for bringing a home made clock to school. To be fair, he shouldn't have worn it strapped to his chest.

You can put off doing anything you set your mind to.

Got my dogs their rabies shots. Now they have dogtism. Great.

At Christmas, I gather up all of the paper and crumple it near my ear. I enjoy listening to wrap.

I once worked at Petco, but was fired for heavy petting.

I went to buy some kielbasa, but took a turn for the wurst.

People say I second guess myself. I mean, maybe I do, but not really. I mean, I just really think about...maybe they're right, maybe.

Don't judge me, person checking my receipt as I'm leaving Costco.

how do they make those collars small enough to fit on a flea

I'm going to start a flattered women's shelter for women who don't take compliments well.

Porn is never the answer. Unless the question is 'what are you watching on the computer?'
Rich: Let's talk astronomy.
Poker Dealer: What sign are you? Rich:
That's astrology.
Poker Dealer: Like the zydeco?
Rich: You mean zodiac.
Poker Dealer:
Rich: Good talk.

Reluctant to Attend the Synagogue On the morning of Rosh Hashanah, Rebecca went into the bedroom to wake her son and tell him it was time to get ready to go to the Shul to which he replied in a dull voice, 'I'm not going.'

'Why not?' Rebecca demanded.

'I'll give you two good reasons Mother,' he said. 'One, they don't like me, and two, I don't like them.'

Riebecca replied in an exasperated voice, 'I'll give you two good reasons why you must go to the synagogue. 'One, you're 54 years old, and two, you're the Rabbi.'
You can count on me, or my name isn't Mark Mywords

I was young and stupid when I was young and stupid.

I sent my picture to a Lonely Hearts dating club. They sent it back saying they weren't that lonely...

Marriage is a relationship in which one person is always right, and the other is a husband.

Did you hear about the baby that was born in a high tech hospital? It came out cordless!

I took an IQ test yesterday. It came back negative...

A recent study found that women who carry a little extra weight live longer than the men who mention it.

I really like selling on E-Bay. Last month I sold my Homing Pigeons eight times!

Two Irishmen were talking: The first asks, "Connor, you know that guy Trump who is running for President?" Connor says, "I do Sean, I do." "Well", says Sean, "The next time he gets up to talk, I'd like to see someone throw a shoe at his head".

"Now, now, you know you're not supposed to wish harm on anyone", says Connor. "Oh!" says Sean, "I'm not wishing him harm, and I just want to see Donald duck." Shoot me now.......

Looking for a partner for todays game, tried to use Gulf Poker site but not accepted yet.

Real eyes realize real lies McDonald's don't make real fries . *snap snap* kill me

Hillary Clinton is someone I could drink a beer with. Bernie Sanders is someone I could smoke a bowl with.

People have been asking me for my recipe for grilled corn, so here it is: 1. Get some corn. 2. Put it on a grill.

Remember me as someone who doesn't want to be remembered for anything.

I've seen fire and rain too but you don't see me writing a song about it.

My "to-do" list has just one thing. As little as possible.

Good Will Space Hunting: "Let's go to a Mahtian bah and fack with some mahtian kids."

Chastity belts are useless if she screwing a locksmith.

"I'll take care of your boils, no charge." "Are you employed by this clinic?" "No, I'm free lancing

Ever gain so much weight after a before picture it becomes an after picture?

Lady at the poker table: "Do you have any idea how handsome you are?"
Rich: "Aw. Thanks."
Lady: "I wish I had my glasses so I could see you better."

I want to get a big dog so that when people on the street ask me, "Who's walking who?" I can whisper "Help me."

Mike Huckabee and Ted Cruz plan to visit that jailed marriage license clerk. I bet she'll still refuse to marry them.

This is not just a Waffle House, its a Waffle Home

My local Waffle House is having a breakfast party for the homeless and less fortunate! They aren't, but it totally looks like it! Good job WH!
As a former Teamster, Labor Day has special significance for me. But I won't share it with you because I'm off the clock.

Consciousness is knowing you know what you know what you know, while you are knowing it.

Never bring a breath mint to a gum fight.

The Internet has given voice to the voiceless...& revealed that many voices were voiceless for good reason

I like to torture my victims with wordplay. I call it pun-ishment.

She got all weird & said we weren't working out as a couple. Imagine my surprise at the empty home when I returned w/ gym memberships.
My GF doesn't want to hear about my past, which is fine, because I don't want to hear about her future.

My psychic business is going bankrupt. I should've seen this coming.

I'm on a tequila diet. I've lost three days already.

"Mr. Wilens, I have reviewed this case very carefully," the divorce court judge said, "and I've decided to give your wife $5275 a month." "That's very fair, your honor," says Rich. "And every now and then I'll try to send her a few bucks myself."

I just ordered a low fat milkshake and nobody was here to witness it.

Life is just like toilet paper. You are either on a roll....or you're mostly taking sh*t from some a**hole.

I'm NOT mean I prefer "Creatively Belligerent" - Tim Castleman

It's time for Tim Tebow to retire. Even Jesus only came back once.

On this day in 1886, Chief Geronimo surrenders to U.S. troops, on the condition that people yell his name when jumping out of airplanes.

Was going to make a herb garden this weekend but I don't have thyme.

GF: Finally got rid of that urn my ex mother in law gave me.
Rich: Was it cathartic?
GF: No, Greek.

Do something today that your future self will pay someone not to reveal.

Anti-marriage equality clerk Kim Davis taken into custody, should be forced to watch entire 8 seasons of ¨Will & Grace" as punishment.

(The following posts took place between November and December 2015. These events did not happen in real time)

August 2015

(sung to the Monkee's Theme song)

Here we come Walkin down the street
We get the funniest looks from
Every one we meet..
Hey Hey were the Junkees

God works in mysterious ways because he doesn't have a boss. If I worked in mysterious ways I'd be fired.

I swallowed my joke book and now my stomach feels funny.

According to the Monkeys' theme song, the only thing preventing them from putting people down was their hectic schedule.
Well call me old fashioned becasue I'm the kind of guy who likes to be called old fashioned.

My superpower is the ability to read my own thoughts.

I want to tell you all about this great sexual experience I had, just as soon as I have it.

What would you serve for dessert at a global warming conference?
Baked Alaska :)

A hundred years ago, a Dollar Store was where rich people shopped.

Your call is important to us. Just not important enough to hire more representatives. Please hold forever.

I was filthy Rich but then I took a shower. Then my GF found out and made me give it back...

If more people thought before they acted then less people would act before they think in response.. I gotta quit smoking that stuff. Oops there's another dollar

I would like to see tennis,played on a huge table.

I was forced to relearn how to find amusing font. I had a full-fontal lobotomy.

Sometimes I spell 'Czech'..........and giggle to myself.

Odd, I don't remember ordering BatShit Crazy for breakfast...

The biggest dilemma of my day is deciding whether or not to post "happy birthday" on someone's Facebook wall

You can't spell Fart without Art. Fact.

What do you call a pony with a sore throat? A little hoarse.

If I had a dollar for every time I've said "I'm never smoking pot again" I would've made 7 dollars this week

Stephen Hawking says black holes lead to other universes.
I just smoked some medicinal bubblegum Kush that does about the same, with no spaceship.

One of the dirtiest items found in a restaurant is the menus, which rarely get wiped down between customers. In response, health officials are urging patrons not to eat anything off the menu.

This is a reminder for those of you who need reminding.

Ashley Madison chief resigns over hacking scandal in order to spend more time with his wife.

I'm going to become a billionaire by inventing a camera that subtracts 10 pounds.

If you want to be great try spending time with people that make you look better by comparison.

Cleanliness is next to godliness in a bad dictionary.

There are three things I can't stand; people who can't count and people who can't spel.

Everybody was Kung Fu fighting. Worst Chinese restaurant I've ever been to.

Told my dog to play dead
and he put on "Truckin'."

I don't know why people keep raving about Mexican Coke. The really good stuff is from Colombia.

Losers quit when they fail. Winners quit while they are ahead.

I just smoked a bowl of some of my "medicinal pot". It's so good my spell check is even like "dude what are you saying?"

The TSA does not find it funny if during your pat down, you take out your airport parking stub and say 'do you guys validate?'

All good things must come to an end. What about bad things? Do they just linger indefinitely?

"You snooze, you lose." -Carbon Monoxide

A shamrock shake is the closest thing I'll ever get to drinking a kale shake...they're both green so technically it's close enough

She loves it when I kiss her with facial stubble but I don't. I prefer that she shaves.

Being indecisive is also a decision.

Ben Affleck had a secret Ashley Madison account using the email address IAmBatman73@gmail.com.

The other day one of those hoax things went around saying that Willie Nelson had died. I sure hope he didn't see it while he was stoned. I can just see him checking his pulse and saying, "What the Hell?!?!"

I just got a text, from an unknown number, that said, "Hey, I'm pregnant. " So I replied, "Hey, me too!"

911: what's your emergency
Rich: It's 8am and I'm drinking shots of tequila
911: sir, that's not a real problem
RICH: *screams at son* 'TOLD YA JAKE'

A group of teenage girls is called a whatev's

Shouldn't taking something "as gospel" mean it's 100% unreliable?

Stephen Hawking: "Black holes are a passage into another universe."
Stripper: "That's great Stevie, but u still owe me $20 for the lap dance

I keep Men's Health magazines around my house to give guests the illusion that I haven't given up yet

Don't worry, former Ashley Madison users, there's still a place where married people go to hook up. It's called 'every other dating site.'

Yep, I helped Jeremiah the Bullfrog drink his wine.

I'm sorry, this is all a bunch of BULLSHIT! Why wasn't my Ashley Madison® account hacked!!?

Sources say Josh Duggar checked himself into rehab for 19 Days and Counting.

Just got my AARP card in the mail. My hands broke out in liver spots and I'm binge watching Murder She Wrote.

I wonder if skunks ever think, "why do I smell like a pound of weed?"

If I were a divorce lawyer, I'd email all 33 million people in the Ashley Madison hack with a coupon.
If there was a trophy for laziness, my son would send me to pick it up.

She's so big, if she sat on an iPhone, it would turn into an iPad.

I miss the days when the internet was just about cybersex in AOL chat rooms, porn, & stealing music, now it's about people's feelings.

I may struggle with wealth, but I am never, ever bankrupt of worth.

Doctor checked my fitness levels and said I'm getting atrophy… I've never won a fitness award before.

"Creator of Undercover Boss goes undercover on production of an episode of Undercover Boss"

"Paternity Test Reveals That Darth Vader is Not Luke's Father" on Maury...

I just read Dr. Scholl's college dissertation and he had some incredible footnotes.

The main difference between genius and stupidity is that stupidity always has more friends.

News reports claims we are the most illiterate generation from the past 100 years. Mind you, I could be reading that wrong.

The Americans & Briton who thwarted train attack received France's top honor, a ménage a trois.

The stock market is tanking so badly, my 401k is now being called a 101k.

I remember when I was a kid, getting an erection in public was very embarrassing. I learned the hard way.

Hey y'all, Message me for details. Details about what? You'll have to message me.

A realistic dating profile for men my age would say "I enjoy peace, quiet, and romantic walks to the bathroom."

I think it's strange that I've been getting lots of spam email asking if I would like to enlarge my penis. Then I find out they been forwarded by my Girlfriend

I always wanted to learn how to juggle… I just never had the balls to do it.
"He's a nice guy once you get to know him." or be honest and say:
"He a dickhead but you'll get used to it."

I think I do pretty good for someone with no talent

First day on the job as a certified pessimist, it could have gone a lot better.

For all the women who say that all men are all the same... How did you manage to try them all?

Remember when you could remember everybody's phone number?

On a scale from 1 to 10, then I'm going to bed.

You're going to give yourself a sex change John? How the hell you going to pull that off?

I'm so lazy when you look at me it's like a still life

GF: Do my ankles look fat?
Rich: Ankles? When did you get ankles?
and that's how that fight started...

I'm neither pro-life or pro-choice. I'm pro-what-a-woman-does-with-her-body-is-none-of-my-business.

I dont understand this. Women want men to talk about their feelings. I told a woman on Facebook that the cleavage in her picture made me feel horny & she blocked me

I really hope Blockbuster is not making a comeback, I'm going to owe a shit load of late fees!!

C'mon Korea, don't make us send Hawkeye, and Hot Lips back over there.

I don't know what's worse - that it takes telemarketers so long to respond to my "Hello?" or that I wait for the response like an idiot.

INTERVIEWER: What's the worst thing you could tell me about yourself, that would 100% tank your chances at getting this job?

I fixed my drinking problem. I joined AA. I still drink, I just go under a different name.

My son Jake is a workaholic. When I mention work, he starts drinking.

I bought my son Jake a bow and arrow for his birthday. He bought me a jacket with a bullseye on the back

My doctor told me last week in his office he had six cases of an std. He's okay now.

Donald Trumps new immigration slogan: you report em' we deport em

I was in in the restroom at the Golden Nugget and I was barely sitting down when I heard a voice in the other stall: "Hi, how are you?" Rich: (embarrassed) "Doin' fine!" Next Stall: "So what are you up to?" Rich: "Uhhh, I'm like you, just sitting here." Next Stall: "Can I come over?" Rich: "No, I'm a little busy right now!!" Next Stall: "Listen, I'll have to call you back. There's an idiot in the other stall who keeps answering all my questions!

I always look for a woman who has a tattoo. I see a woman with a tattoo, and I'm thinking, okay, here's a girl who's capable of making a decision she'll regret in the future.

"Mr. DiCaprio, why is your face so white?" "I'm on a pale Leo diet I posted worse.....(:(

Let me see if I get this. People get MRSA from hospitals. MRSA spread due to overuse of antibiotics. So doctors prescribe antibiotics just in case you might have MRSA.

So many guys should be showing their wives the Ashley Madison list to go "See! I'm not on there!"

Jared, I have some advice for you. On your 1st day in prison find the most dangerous inmate, walk right up to him & threaten 2 write the warden a sternly written note about him.

Hackers are now threatening to expose Netflix members who have watched Billy Madison.

(The following posts took place between November and December 2015. These events did not happen in real time)

July 2015

Guys my age: Break the viagra into quarters; 4 hours will kill you

I can't afford Ashley Madison. I joined Oscar Madison. It's messy

As long as they don't hack Gratuitous Grannies, I'm fine

There's a fine line between living in the moment

Upside for Ashley Madison users? If the entire world knows what you're doing, then it's not called "cheating."

The good thing about having multiple personalities is that you always have someone to talk to.

I get nervous when naked in front of a woman for the first time. More so when the server at KFC tells me this won't help get extra fries

There's a special place in hell for people who hold doors open for you while you're a mile away. Do I look like I want to run?

I wonder where Donald Trump stands with Juggalo voters

When Jared Fogle goes to prison, all the inmates will eat fresh.

Rich: Dammed! The dog drank my beer!
GF: Go get another one!
Rich: I'm sure the pet store closed right now!

Being a numbskull sounds like it would be relaxing.

Everyone has this internal conflict in their life: Part of me says stop smoking pot, the other says, don't listen to that guy, he's stoned.

A raspberry is just a berry with a sore throat.

I walked a dog today that was tired and done after half a block. He is my spirit animal.

GF: How did I end up so lucky to be with a wonderful man like you?
Rich: I lost the bet.

Sweep the leg. Mop the calf. Swiffer the kneecap. Sponge the thigh.

Oh. My. God. Becky, look at his personal brand. It is sooo big. Like one of those IM Gurus who friends Rap guys...

my dog Reggie leaves the couch only when there's food involved - clearly takes after me

On Thursday the F.D.A. may approve the first drug to improve a woman's sex drive, because technically money isn't a drug.

In the end, always love a woman for her personality... If you very lucky, she might have several to chose from.

I broke it off with my blow up doll girlfriend, I just felt like things between us were falling flat.

I used to date a witch. She always ordered burnt steaks.

Hangover cure: Weed, burrito, orgasm, nap. Unrelated tip for women in Biloxi: I have weed and know a good burrito joint.

I bought a paint bucket, a mop bucket, and a bucket of beer. Now I can scratch three things off my bucket list.

A Pastor in McMinnville, Tennessee is blaming "liberal society" for banning the stoning of gay people here in the US. Thats crazy. I know for a fact there are gays in Colorado and Washington state getting stoned this very moment.

Pulling out your back while sleeping is God's way of saying "Rich I give you 8 hours to do nothing and you can't even handle that"

Hosting a charity event for those with sexual dysfunction Please RSVP me if you can't come

Everyone has that one friend that always says "I gotta guy." We get it; you're gay. It's cool now. It's 2015.

I like to walk into a pool hall, and see a bunch of tight racks.

When I was younger, I was in a parking garage band. We were never really validated.

If KFC is hiring ex-SNL stars to be Colonel Sanders, they should put up a picture of Chris Farley to show what happens after you eat KFC.

The Jar Jar Binks ride at Disney's Star Wars parks will be modeled after It's a Small World so you'll want to kill yourself even faster.

The colonoscopy camera is now regarded as the first ever selfie stick.

If Caitlyn Jenner get diabetes......would he be a "Sweet Transvestite?"

Watching "Intervention." It's amazing. This girl inhales up to 10 cans of computer duster a day yet her keyboard is still filthy!

Turns out my company doesn't like misery.

Congrats to Mark Zuckerberg and Priscilla Chen who are having a baby... it seems after several pokes she finally accepted his friend request.

Hillary's personal emails contain sensitive information. John McCain's telegraph tape reveals the Spanish American War was an inside job

There are mallard ducks who spend the majority of their time in front of a mirror practicing their teenage girl lips.

Rich: You're married aren't you.
Woman at Poker Table: I'm not wearing a ring, how'd you know?
Rich: You look miserable.

When nothing is impossible prove them wrong by doing nothing at all.

I love to tell people about how I met my GF at a seedy massage parlor.
It's a great story with a happy ending.

Sometimes I tell myself I should cut down on my pot smoking. But I realize I am no way near stoned enough to be having this conversation.

Since I'm still single, I never make the same mistake, once.

She wanted to watch 'Scent of a Woman' So I did a search on Netflix and the first pick on the list was, "A Fish Called Wanda" weird

My GF bought a musical dildo that plays, "You got a friend in me"

I took a load of my old things to a garage sale today. I've never had so many people feeling my junk.

You cant judge a hooker by her shoes. Just saying g-nite folks Today is a new day that I still haven't used the word "homie" to describe a white Facebook friend.

Sound of Music the movie, is totally perverse. In what other movie have you heard people singing about doing a female deer?

I'm going to stand on a street corner while holding a sign that says "PLEASE HELP! Working class white man living paycheck-to-paycheck!"

Whatever your wife wants, it will never be enough.

My GF amazes me how she can have a long conversation and not require me to pretend to listen.

Rock paper scissors duct tape shovel rope. - DIY abduction

I have a fetish for terminally ill women, I just can't pass up a limited time offer. it's ok you can boo

I haven't been "getting laid" so I like to work my frustrations out at the gym. Nothing like reliving yourself watching women do yoga.

After calling the Iraq War "a pretty good deal'....Jeb Bush now says he was confusing it with Amazon Prime

My dogs version of twerking is dragging his ass across the carpet.

Doctor Olsen: Have you been having sex regularly?
Rich: No Doc, I'm into some serious kinky stuff.

Why do some people believe motivation comes from destruction and pain? Come on, seriously, isn't getting hemorrhoids bad enough?

Why would you take the term "Idiot Proof" as a personal challenge??

At the poker table, I blew my nose so hard that the person next to me farted.

40 years ago today is when "The Rocky Horror Picture Show" premiered in the U.K. I feel like doing the Time Warp again. Actually I would rather be a sweet transvestite From Transexual, Transylvania.

Scientists has determined that living trees actually make noises when they are running out of water, just like a person gasping for air when it's in short supply. I haven't heard any noises from the tree outside my window, but it has tried to text me a few times and not surprisingly, some of those messages were pretty sappy.

I've heard that moderation is the key to whether you can drink alcohol while dieting and still lose weight. You bet you can! Why a steady diet of vodka, cocaine, Xanax and Marlboro Lights and you'll be in that Dad bod before you can utter the words "rehab!"

Why would you settle for a bunch of grapes when you can get a case of wine?

Happy Left-Handers' Day, spawn of Satan!

Disney show about kids growing up poor called, "That's So Ramen"

I was lame before it was cool

The definition of loneliness is watching Maury, seeing them flash back to a previous episode, and going, "Oh yeah, I remember that one."

Alfonso Ribeiro wanted to call Will Smith about the Fresh Prince of Bel-Air reboot, but he's out of minutes on his prepaid cell phone.

Damn illegal immigrants coming here and putting billions into the social security system without being able to collect those benefits

Al Gore is not running for president. Stating the timing is wrong with an ice age right around the corner and the sun about to explode.

If the leader of Russia grew dreads, would he be Rasputin?

Victoria's Secret? She once killed a drifter.

Losing isn't an option unless I'm being realistic about my limited abilities.

It's a good thing I'm not a violin player because I don't know how to play the violin.

Tinder? I barely even know her!

What type of personality did Fonzie have? Type Ayyyyyy.

I'd love to see a meatier shower.

Pepsi launches a version of their Diet soda without Aspartame. The secret ingredient this time is just straight up cancer.

Cannabis residue is found on Shakespeare's 400 yr-old tobacco pipes -proving you DO have to be high to understand it

He's directing the orchestra AND he's first violin in the orchestra? I don't like the way he's conducting hims.......no no no stop the insanity

I'm starting a gofundme campaign to help offset my Starbucks expenses

The secret to a long happy marriage is just another secret.

It's funny I remember as a kid saying I wanted to grow up and every adult saying "trust me you don't" I really get it now.

Coca Cola blames obesity on the lack of exercise. Well played, can of liquid sugar. Well played.

I wish my girlfriend was made of pizza and not just made up.

In Germany the Walmart greeters stare at you menacingly and ask you for your papers.

If you mention that a certain group of people are "part of the problem" then YOU'RE part of the problem.

Can't wait to become a U.S. citizen so I can finally travel to Mexico & get affordable dental care.

The saddest thing about being named Stewart is when people spell it 'Stuart' and you have to correct them.

My greatest fear is suffering a heart attack while playing charades

Megyn Kelly is a journalist, like Donald Trump is a hair model.

Local Alzheimer Support Group held a romantic evening of dancing for couples. It was billed as: "A Night You Won't Remember"

If I had a dollar for every pimple I've ever had, it could change the whole complexion of my life.

Eating a puppy on TV while wearing a cap that says "F*ck The Troops" is the only thing Trump could do that would hurt his poll numbers. (Maybe)

How many people with OCD does it take to change a lightbulb? It depends on their body weight and windspeed.

Donald Trump threatens to run as a third party candidate as a member of the Whig Party.

Sent my goldfish to school to become a sturgeon.

What do we want? Time travel! When do we want it? Years ago!

My GF asked me to show her the world. So I bought her a globe.

I like jazz so much I watch porn for the music.

I live next door to two lesbians who never close their drapes. I'm not sure where I'm going with this, so I thought I brag about it.

An Indian restaurant that's naan profit

There a couples seminar for those who are having difficulties satisfying their partner. I can't get her to come.

Do people into bondage get turned on by restraining orders?

(The following posts took place between November and December 2015. These events did not happen in real time)

June 2015

My GF has a coffee mug that says "I don't do mornings". I wrote "Or her BF" underneath in sharpie.

GF: What would you do if your superpower was shooting lightning from your fingers?
Rich: I'd masturbate more carefully.

I figure out what's wrong with my internet router. I took it to the IT guy and the router told him, "It hurts when IP"

Got my 10000 steps in today. Not sure it counts if I was just walking from meal to buffet to snack to meal to Jamba Juice to Taco Bell to......

A new study has determined that exercise and not diet has the most impact on weight as we age. Yea, well its not my fault that Cheesecake factory doesn't have exercise equipment.

Fried eggs are just eggs that have taken too much LSD.

Violence against women is never okay, except when it's carried out by Ronda Rousey. Then it's awesome.

My uncle was caught stealing a Walmart air conditioner. He is currently Freon bail.

Two Asian food trucks decided to street race. The race wound up being a Thai.

AdamSandler will undergo Tommy John Surgery. He needs to have his funny bone replaced.

The Bad News:The funeral home burned down. The Good News:Everyone gets a free cremation!

I walked into a Nordstrom Rack and I thought to myself "oh, ladies, I get it."

Being bipolar is like being happy someone just gave you an amazing gift but you simultaneously throw it back in their face while yelling

International Cat Day This is why other Universes don't take us seriously.

I wonder if the Pope,has a papal Paypal account.

True Detective's Ratings Continue to Fall Steadily. They've hired detectives to investigate why.

I justify all-you-can-eat buffets as an educational expense. I'm finding out how much I can eat.

My new product is an app that connects you with people who look exactly like your ex: Twinder

A modern version of The Angels' song "My Boyfriend's Back" would go, "My boyfriend's back and he's going to blog about you." or My boyfriends black and there's gonna be trouble..... (sing it)

Sometimes I'll flush the toilet & then start to pee just to see who wins

Officer: "You're under arrest for trying to steal an iPad." Rich: "But officer, my doctor told me I had to take one tablet a day."

Did every animal on Earth live with in walking distance to Noah's Boat?

Don't sweat it or regret it... Just move on and forget it.

I hate it when the police pulls me over to criticize my driving. Bad enough to hear it from the passengers.

When you get to be my age, you stop asking yourself if you are doing it right. You now ask yourself if it's almost over.

Office Air Conditioning Is Biased Against Women: A new study is suggesting that temperature settings on office air conditioners may be biased against women. I thought that could be the case after I noticed the settings on the thermostat read warm, cool and freeze bitch."

Debate questions I want to hear: Do you think 'Urkel',is the only black Republican? Does a Donald trump a Jeb? Will Texas allow 'Taco Bell',to make a run for the border? How much of the Matrix Trilogy is nonfiction? Who here is pissed off they didn't get to shoot the lion?

Several people have recommended I read Eckhart Tolle's "The Power of Now." And I will. Eventually.

You ever just roll out of bed and feel like "shit I have to do this again"

My bologna has a first name because I anthropomorphize my lunch meats.

It's not you, it's me, lying about how it's not you.

My GF and I made a deal to quit smoking. We would smoke one cigarette each time we had sex. I have the same pack since 2011 What bothers me, if she's up to four packs a day.

I'm the Pink Lady and Jeff of obscure references. (anyone? lol)

I'm at that age where people say He's at that age......IDGAF about that either lol

Jake bitches at me when I'll walk in through an out door. IDGAF.

Just once I'd like to flaunt my butthole at my cat.

If your rat wears a long white coat it's probably a lab rat.

If you think you're a baby cat you're only kitten yourself.
Roses are red, Violets are blue, Daddy Hulk might have said the N-word, But at least he's not a Jew. -Brooke Hogan's 1st Draft

Ice T and Coco are expecting their first child together. They'll name it Grape Soda if it's a boy and Fanta if it's a girl.

When the moon hits your eye like a big pizza pie, that's the acid kicking in.

If we don't defund Planned Parenthood, where will we get the next generation of unwanted kids to grow up and make our prisons profitable?

Maybe Kermit was trying to tell us something when he sang "The Rainbow Connection."

Why Is It that we can put a man on the moon but we can't put an apostrophe in a hashtag

Imagine how different poetry would be if it were: Roses are red, violets aren't...

We all should write down the unwritten rules so they is no future arguments.

You are your solution. You are your motivation. You are also your biggest problem.

I overheard a lesbian couple order boneless chicken at KFC. Funny

Phoenix Airport Security: has anyone put anything in your luggage without your knowledge, sir? Rich: How the hell am I supposed to answer that?

Ronda Rousey fights like a black woman who thinks a white woman is checking out her man.

I'm only putting myself through college so I can be a stripper.

The first rule about being a mime is you don't tell anyone you're a mime
I'd like some crab legs but I can't afford the surgery.

Punctuation is very important. "Bob And His Big Dog, Dick," is different than "Bob And His Big Dog Dick."

I always want to inspire people. I want someone to look at me and say, " It was because of you, I turned around and went the other way."

I always thought the phrase "nice guys finished last" was a sexual reference. Man, was I wrong.

If you're bisexual and live in North America, chances are, ½ of your parents will still love you...

I ask myself constantly "what the hell am I reading this for?" Then I realize I'm on Facebook and all my friends are idiots.

Can an illegal immigrant perform a citizen's arrest?

I was an underwear model until they arrested me.

I broke up with my online girlfriend due to a connection failure

This just in: Tony the Tiger was stabbed by a Michigan Podiatrist.....

Your heads would explode if Cecil the Lion was buried in a Confederate flag.

It's National Girlfriend Day and I have no idea how I'm going to pull this one off because I have plans with my wife today.

Maybe next time, you'll think twice asking one of your coworkers to book your safari to hunt lions.

Today, I woke up feeling great. So I immediately went on Facebook on my phone and put a stop to that

Just updated my relationship status to "please keep it down I'm napping"

I can hear my religious neighbors having sects

I heard about this stuff called 'cannabis butter'. I think it's supposed to keep your pot from sticking.

I'll say it once and I'll say it again: I hate repeating myself

Parents, don't worry about teaching your kids about sex. Teach them the difference between affect and effect.

Knowledge is appreciating how beautiful she is... Wisdom is buying sunglasses when visiting a nude beach together.

She tells me I'm impossible to please… I wasn't happy to hear that.

At this point, pretty much everyone is better than ezra.

A service that will drive your potato to its destination called Tuber.

When you open a bag of M&M's do you eat the M's first or the M's?

One time I typed "your" instead of "you're", and immediately went into contractions.

She asked me what my sine was. I said,"You do the math!"

I give Koreans wrong directions, just to disorient them.

National Geographic is pretty hip. They were featuring a gay pride of lions.

I was attacked by a murder of Velcrows. This has always stuck with me.

Some of the Children of the Corn, grew up to be military kernels. The 'Elephant Man' was known to live out of his trunk.

Her name was Ha Choo. But she was nothing to sneeze at.

According to Master Baiter Fishing Magazine, sperm whales are most attracted to jail bait

I put the "taco" AND the "coma" in Tacoma.

Netflix added a new Scottish movie called : No Country For Auld Men

My periodic table has a chemical imbalance. The "Ho" is completely out of control.

Women complain that sex is the only thing men want... It's not true, we also want the remote control.

If you let me into your dreams, I'll make them come true.

I read this book on Narcissism. I swear this book was written about me.

Maybe I will stop being fat if I work on being taller.

I had a wet dream recently, but not the kind you're thinking. This one was about sex.

If you're like most people, then like most people, you don't know you're like most people... wait, what?

Antman is hung like a gnat.

What stays in Vegas, ya right....Here's what just happened to me...... I saw a gas station in here in Las Vegas with a HUGE sign saying "Free Sex with Fill-up." I pulled in, filled my tank, and then asked for my free sex. The blonde attendant gave me a ticket for the free sex and told me to go down the hall and through the door. I was so excited I couldn't believe it. I walked down the hall and thru the door and there was this Bouncer type guy standing there with a handful of tickets. I said are you the ticket taker... He say's No, I'm Phillip.....

Paul Rudd is an uncle who wears his wife's clothes in "Aunt-Man."

And it seems to me you lived your life like a
Kindle in the wind.

I love having sex in public places... Anyone else care to join in?

I'm a Metro-sexual.....I only have sex during Met games

Hurricanes are given women names only because they like to come in wild and wet. Then they leave you, taking the house and car.

Donald Trump reveals Lindsey Graham's cell phone number as 867-5309.

I paid a visit to the Cheers pub in Boston, but nobody knew my name!

A bee that drugs other bees in order to have sex with them is called a Cosbee.

Rich: Why are you holding both your hands over your ears...
Do you have a headache?
GF: No. I'm trying to hold onto a thought.

Donald Trump kicks homeless man's dog; his lead in the polls among GOP candidates spikes.

(The following posts took place between November and December 2015. These events did not happen in real time)

May 2015

I adopted a highway so I can drive like I own the road....

deletes browser history What's Ashley Madison?

You're really out of shape if you fart and suddenly need a nap.

Well, I finally got around to asking my doctor about Lipitor and the only thing he could say was "How did you find out where I live?"

When I asked the ATM for my checking balance it did a drum roll.

Oh, you have a blog AND a podcast. Pardon me while I just go over here and hang myself.

Michigan legislators are proposing a tax on legalized marijuana to pay for road repairs. I'd call it Potheads for Potholes.

[At a funeral] Rich: If u need ANYTHING, just ask.
Bereaved: Buy me a golf cart. Rich: Bereaved: And a cotton candy machine.
Rich: But..
Bereaved: U said anything

Rich: I'll have that Corvette.
Salesman: But you don't have any money.
Rich: I know. But I identify as rich.

My dandruff is getting worse. I leaned over the fish tank and they thought it was feeding time...

Where's the hospital that hires all the strippers who finally graduated from nursing school?

Conversation at the poker table tonight:
Where'd you go to college?"
I studied abroad.
"What was she like?"
Who?
"The broad."

I asked the person taking my order: Can you tell me if your "Chicken Wings Family Pack" means it feeds the whole family or it consists of a specific chicken family?
(silence)
(more silence)
I'll ask the manager......

I know I'm getting old when I wake up and I hear a strange noise, and then realize it's my breathing. Damn

Render unto Caesar, croutons, Parmesan cheese, lemon juice, olive oil, egg, Worcestershire sauce, garlic and black pepper.

Superman is NOT a hero. He's just a violent alien who sneaked into this planet illegally." -- Donald Trump

If you can't fix it with duct-tape then it's definitely her problem.

Would you kindly stop talking and, "puff puff pass".. the rule is always puff puff pass.

Jurassic Park, only instead of dinosaurs it's aging rock stars.

The three Australian brothers who are window washers are called the Squee Gees.

Some mistakes are way too much fun to only happen once.

Anybody else dance for a living? In fact, where do strippers train. In Poland...Pole land..Get it...Good nite Gracie

Jared Fogle was cut from Sharknado III because of mere suspicions. We already know Michele Bachmann's an idiot but she's still in it.

Fun Sports Facts: Tennis great Bjorn Borg,had a brother named Cy.

I'm jealous of people who only encounter loneliness at at the top

If a Cockapoo is a cross between a Cocker Spaniel and a Poodle, what is a cross between a Bulldog and Shih tzu called?

If Ant-Man fought The Fly, it would almost be insectuous.

If it wasn't for futility, I'd get no exercise at all

Women seem to think men will screw anything that moves... That totally sexist and untrue! It doesn't have to move.

3 out of 4 doctors recommend whoever gives them free shit.

Trying to get out of my own way is the hardest thing I have ever attempted.

Now that I've seen Pluto I'd really like to see Uranus.

I just bought the entire country of Greece on Amazon PrimeDay......Now what?

I used to think the only thing that could put me to sleep was a little pot and some vallum then I watched the MLB all star game......

When I ordered at Starbucks this morning, I told them my name was Mike H u n t. Thats how to start your morning.

If Batman smoked an e-cig he'd be the Vaped Crusader.

I thought an antacid was a hallucinogenic for bugs.

I wish that I had Jessie's girl explain to me why nobody knows her name.

Cee Lo Green is my favorite Minion.

Satoru Iwata, President of Nintendo, died this weekend, and consequently must start all over from the first level again.

Relationships would be far easier if it came with a Clear History button.

What if life doesn't even give you lemons?

Jake Wilens: Sorry, Dad. I'm a DJ now. I can mix loud and hard and there's nothing you can do to stop me.
Rich: [unplugs turntables]

I put ketchup condiment package under the GF's back wheels. I waited for her to back the car up and then I screamed, "OH MY GOD, YOU KILLED THE CAT **no more GF btw (looking)**

I really regret getting this memory-foam mattress. It's been 10 years since I got divorced and it's STILL playing back arguments it heard.

Rich: It looks great on you. The colour really nice and... GF: I can tell there's a big 'but' coming. Rich: You said it, I did'nt.

I ain't saying she's a gold digger, but she yells "do not resuscitate!" every time her husband trips over something.

I started working out at this private gym where everyone there is gorgeous. It's ironic that I try to raise my self esteem at a place that kills my self esteem

Here in Biloxi, a young man was found dead in a botched attempt in circumcision. The police have no leads, and are asking the public for tips.

Just wait till you read the "Catcher in the Rye" sequel w/ an older, wisecracking Holden Caulfield turning tricks as a street hustler in LA.

I love Twitter, I love that you love twitter, I love... wow, this is really good shit.. uh, coffee!

I'm doing a book signing at the Biloxi Barnes & Noble. Bring your favorite book cuz I haven't written any.

I'm much too famous locally to accept your Facebook friend request.

You know you got a hearing problem when you talk to yourself and say "what?"

Discretion is the better part of valor. It also stops you from wearing a speedo to the beach.

GF: I'm back from the Beauty Salon!
Rich: Aww, sorry babe, why was it closed?

The only Latino voting for Donald Trump is Geraldo Rivera.

The Confederacy shall not rise again. The flag is down. We lost. Again.

I heard two women talking in the Waffle House and one tells the other: "Just cut off 4 inches of hair, that's soooo long" I like the way she describes 4 inches, we'd be a perfect match

Ant Man is no match for Magnifying Glass Kid!

First thing on my list of things to do today; Make list.\

Jeb Bush said that Americans need to work "longer hours". Can someone explain to this bozo that an hour can't be any longer than 60 minutes?

Drinking large quality of booze can cause memory loss... Or worst, memory loss

Ever wrapped yourself in toilet paper and walked around groaning and saying that you have a mummy ache? Bada boom

Which celebrities give the best medical advice?

How do Scientists freshen their breath? With Experi-Mints!

Ben Gay has married Uncle Ben. Converted rice was thrown,at the first gay product wedding.

I love my new meds. It makes English my second language and It takes 2 hours to watch 60 minutes.

I have no luck with women. I called this girl last night. I thought we hit it off. She told me to come over nobody's home. I went over, nobody was home.....

You start out with one luftballon and before you know it you have 99 of them.

"I yam what I yam!" - Popeye, if he were a yam.

What type of knife would a vampire never use? A stake knife. Thank you.

Caught my dog wearing a cat collar again.

Saturday in the park I think, it was the 4th of July

People love to give the finger, on the 4th of July. Some of them give two or three.

A pervert got arrested watching my GF undress through the bedroom window… Apparently the police said he couldn't stop screaming.

"Two heads are better than one" is undeniable proof that men, have the potential to think with both of them.

All this debate about being Transracial makes me embarrassed to be a black man.

What's all this talk of the Red Sox having no offense? I watch them play... They are very offensive!!

I'm thinking of starting a new league made entirely of suspended NFL players.

Enjoy the little things in life she says. Big things come in small package she says. Oh my god it's so big! She says.

Today, I went with my BMI.

Have you ever notice amateur porn stars look like your neighbours?

I used to be a drifter, but I eventually straightened up.

My phone's screen is extra sticky because I just finished pleasuring myself* *eating ice cream

If you still get 4G is it camping?

Location Biloxi Mississippi. Golden Nugget. Almost fourth of July.... What is more American than an +++ larger woman in her 50's, wearing a Save the Whale tank top, on an Oxygen tank at a slot machine, with a confederate flag on her mobility scooter that has a gun rack, smoking a cigarette while preaching how American health care is the best. Yup

What's the best way to chop up a body? Axing for a friend.

I personally don't like the term ally, I'd prefer being called a confederate.

'be true to yourself' is the worst advice.

I can't decide. Should I buy a Tempur-Pedic mattress or a car? WTF is buried in that mattress, GOLD?

There's a right way to do things & then there's the left way.
Read my lips. Translate my eyebrows. Modulate my mustache. Inscribe my earlobes. Transmogrify my nose.

Will Smith will not be in the Independence Day sequel because according to his agent he doesn't star in hit movies anymore.

What has a $40,000 income, ten fingers, and twelve years of schooling? 5 rednecks playing with fireworks.

Spider-Man is in the next Captain America. I haven't been this excited about a crossover since the Green Acres/Petticoat Junction mash up.

I also believe in traditional marriage which is why I will allow you to marry my 13 year old daughter but i will only give you two goats.

The shittiest palindrome has to be poop.

Whenever I see an emotional, heart wrenching TV spot sponsored by the Ad Council, my first reaction is always "Wtf is the Ad Council?"

Using The Dukes of Hazard to defend your opinion of the Confederate flag is like using Jello Pudding to defend your opinion of rape.
Anytime my doctor tells me I'm overweight I remind him that it's okay because I "identify" as a skinny person

Ben Affleck and Jennifer Garner file for divorce after ten years. No word yet on if they will split custody of Matt Damon.

I went to Alabama and all I got was a paternity test. Roll tide...

Goldfish initially get excited when freeing them from the tank to sit with you on the couch, but eventually they tire and fall asleep.

Anyone else notice that Caitlyn Jenner looks a lot like Bruce Jenner?

In 10 years' time people who currently like Lady Gaga and One Direction will make decisions about your health care. Sleep well.

I can't hide it anymore; I am a sex worker. I work to make money so I can take a girl out for dinner in the hopes she'll sleep with me.

Can I carry on without keeping calm?

(The following posts took place between November and December 2015. These events did not happen in real time)

April 2015

Since Obamacare, if you fall off the ladder and break both legs, you are fully covered if you go to a walk-in clinic.

I'm beginning to understand how difficult stalkers can be. Everyplace I go, there she is 20 steps ahead of me.

If Gluten, Lime Disease, West Nile, Ozone, salt, pesticides, fluoride and 2nd hand smoke were "deadly", where's my disability pension?

The lesbian mayor of Houston is so excited about gay marriage, she is currently somewhere over the rainbow.

The number one wedding song at gay marriages is: It's Raining Men At Lesbian weddings: Man, I feel like a woman!

So, to sum things up: Confederate flags are out, rainbow flags are in.

In other amazing news Gayle and Oprah just registered at Michaels..

I'm so dumb I thought one of the benefits of being gay was you didn't have to get married. ;)

I'm not insecure, why would you say that about me? What do you know, and who told you I'm insecure? I'm not, I'm paranoid, get it right.

Wow. All I can say is... That's SO Raven!

Is anyone really a true detective?

Finally a law that doubles your chances of marriage...

Louisiana Governor Bobby Jindal announced his candidacy for (yawn) never mind.

Wal-Mart to stop selling Confederate flag merchandise. One shopper noted, "you can take my flag, but you'll never take my truck nuts."

I'm getting really really lazy. I just let a YouTube ad play out in its entirety.

I like my soy milk the way I like women's breasts. Fake with no real milk inside.

Dustin Diamond sentenced to 4 months in jail for stabbing. That's bad news. The other inmates are looking forward to making him screech.

Pete Rose may have placed bets as a player. That may be true. However, it's still not as bad as hitting a woman or using steroids.

The Guinness Book of World Records holds the record for Least Necessary Book.

I've booked a webinar where porn stars teach people how to use social media. Nice Power Point..

As Pete Rose was trying to say, he never bet on games as a player, except the ones he bet on. Jeez, let him finish his sentence!

She asked me what my sine was. I said, "You do the math!"

I'm a morning person. My mornings just start at noon....

if your wife or GF ask you if you've slept with another women don't reply, "since when?" Not a good idea...

If you say that humanity is the only intelligent life in the universe I challenge you to define intelligence.

I've never watched an episode of Hoarders, but I've recorded all 4 seasons onto VCR tapes and boxed them up in the garage.

What did we do before the internet? Wait, let me google that.

If you contract a virus from visiting Facebook, you have given your computer a social disease.

To-do list if you're stuck in the desert: 1) Name your horse.

Guy Fieri is what would happen if a cold sore came to life.

Way to ruin the surprise, Spanish exclamation points.

Went to the Naval Academy so I could study belly buttons.
"How do you spell your name?" "Y-O-U-R-N-A-M-E."

The worst dressed Hardy Boy has to be Ed.

I got fired from the Orange Juice factory because I couldn't concentrate....

I used to be a human cannonball but I kept getting fired.

Guys named Cliff are always on the edge.

For Father's Day, my kids are treating me to the co-pay on my blood pressure meds.

Happy Father's day to half the guests on the Maury Povich show.

To the Dads who abandoned their family's & never came home after going out for a pack of cigarettes - Way to keep your kids from smoking. Happy Father's Day

Happy Father's Day, and, more importantly, Happy, Your Not-The-Father's Day!
My listicles are so sore today.

You can put "The other singer in Wham!" on your résumé and no one will question it.

Someone gave me a copy of the Best of Nickelback and the CD was blank.

Here are some things I'm never gonna do: 1. Give you up. 2. Let you down. 3. Run around and desert you.

I'm declaring a moratorium on using the word moratorium.

If you hook up with a depressed cross-eyed girl... She will never look forward to anything.

The doctor said that my heavy marijuana use was making me paranoid... Doc: When did you have your last toke? Me: What do you MEAN, LAST?

My Twitter account is a classic example of supply and demand. I supply bad tweets, and people demand I stop.

No one named Seymour is under 70 years old.

Say what you want about mimes, they won't respond.

I'm often mistaken for a black woman due to my sassiness.

What do you call a dress that's worn by a cow? A muumuu.

Million dollar idea: Get a billion dollars. Invest poorly.

I think I may pot too much smoke.

CANADIAN ROBBERY Robber: Gimme all your money! Victim: [raises eyebrows expectantly] Robber: I'm sorry. Please give me all of your money.

I'm in shape. It's squishy & round but it's a shape.

They were actually W & W's until the secret formula was stolen.

What do you call a piece of pork that knows martial arts? A Karate Chop.

Currently casting for a homemade porno about spy's. Email me with subject line "James Bondage"

The number one item on my bucket list is meeting Ben and Jerry and giving both a big kiss.

Watching them film The Real Trailer Park Wives of Alabama at the Golden Nugget tonight.....bless their hearts.....

I go to the gym for the free wifi

My American dream involves $2 million (after taxes) & being lazy. I'm half way there. Anyone got $2 million?

I can't handle the truth because the truth has no handles.

GF: What would you regret most if you were to die in your sleep?
Rich: Probably coming to bed.

Admit it, guys. You had a moment when you first saw Caitlyn. Then it hit you. But u still had the moment. And that's in your head now.

Damnit, this can of whoop ass is past its expiration date.

I keep pressing the F5 key but I don't feel refreshed.

"Sorry, I lost that number." - Rikki.

How much wang could a wang chung chung if a wang chung could chung wang?

I'm proud to say, no NBA player has ever dunked on me.

My CPAP machine makes it hard for me to participate in orgies.

Me: I can't do that
Alcohol: Yes you can.

It bugs me when when I'm talking and someone interrupts me to say I'm too controlling, when clearly it's not their turn to speak.
I already feel bad for the kids that will grow up & find out their baby pics only got 12 likes.

Having trouble finding a good person to write my autobiography.

Interviewer: Under weaknesses you say you're too accommodating.
Me: I can change that if you like.

Are all hulks incredible or just that one

Hey, Jeb Bush! Would publicly shaming unwed mothers apply to Mary who was unmarried when she got knocked up with the son of God?

Oscar Pistorius is set to be released on parole on August 21. He will definitely not be made to wear an ankle bracelet.

After 1,000 years the Kama Sutra book is now being updated. Sex positions to include sitting naked in front of computer.

Lifting weights is a great stress reliever but so is shoveling cookie dough ice cream down my throat

When you gaze long into the bisque the bisque also gazes into you

Marriage is the multiplayer mode of life.

I come from a long line of conga dancers.

Maybe the dinosaurs became extinct because they were on the Paleo Diet.

If at first you don't succeed, go back to bed.

Give a man a fish and he'll eat for a day. Teach a man to fish and he'll be saddled with crippling student loans for decades.

"Wow, what happened to you?" I got beat up by Ann and Nancy Wilson. "So, you're saying it was..." A Heart attack.

American Pharaoh had 37 Fillies waiting for him at the stable. And 2 Kardashians...

Those are the Republican presidential hopefuls? I thought they were filming The Expendables IV.

Send in the Clowns, I'll pay extra...

Can't wait until I die so I can start spinning in my grave.

The key to making a good Long Island Iced Tea is to not use a lot of Long Island.

Yesterday was National Donut Day. Today is "National I Promise to Start My Diet Tomorrow Day."

Caitlyn Jenner says she's "the new normal." How many rich former Olympian old ladies w/ a show full of vapid whorish daughters do you know?

If you're gonna be mediocre, strive for consistency.

My first marriage, I once spent months planning the most extravagant proposal imaginable but I was too tired so I got her pregnant instead.

Someone got offended at my homeless joke and said "hey I have a homeless friend"...clearly not that good of a friend if he's still homeless

Autocorrect has been around for a few years now, I got mine when I got a new GF.

Jake: Dad? How do you know when you've met the right girl?
Dad: They'll tell you son.

GF: if I had a penis, I'd play with it all the time.
Rich : Well, here you go.

True laziness is being excited when plans get canceled.

I love oxygen. It's in my blood.

Got thrown out of Golden Corral for bathing in the chocolate fountain again.

What if I don't want to be a G. Can I be a different letter?

I went to college for a year before getting thrown out for not being a student there.

Kris Jenner claims to be inspired by Caitlyn Jenner to also transition to a woman.

Johnny Manziel threw a water bottle at a heckling fan, which was promptly intercepted and returned for a touchdown (and 5¢ in Iowa).

How is one supposed to work out when Ben and Jerry's keeps inventing new flavors?

Do we really need more than one way to skin a cat?

I have an idea for an app which will calibrate the number of calories of food in pictures posted on Instagram. It's called Fat Shamer.

A mop that cleans up for you after a failed relationship called a Taylor Swiffer.

If you've never used electricity before you're in for quite a shock.

HBO to premier companion series to Hard Knocks about NFL cheerleaders titled "Hard Knockers"

(The following posts took place between November and December 2015. These events did not happen in real time)

March 2015

If Jesus had true twit validation he'd have known Judas was a fake account.

92-year-old becomes oldest woman to finish a marathon. However, she started the race when she was 90

How long before people start calling Caitlyn Jenner a TILF? :)

What a lovely surprise to finally discover how un lonely being alone can be.

I want to advise you about taking advice on Twitter. This may or may not count.

Wait. I found a loophole! If we actually pay the mortgage .. we can keep the house.

Guys, I just saw the Rolling Stones tour bus! It was on the highway going 35mph in the left lane with the blinker on.

It's a little-known fact that Jack Nicholson and I have won a total of three Oscars between us.

I have been playing so much poker lately, whenever I leave the bathroom I always say "Seat Open"

Rich: I can't believe you lost $300, what were you thinking.
GF: Why are you yelling at me, you lost over $3,000.
Rich: Yeah!, But I know how to gamble!

Rich Wilens: Wanna hear a bad joke about a parking ticket?
GF: No!
Rich: Fine!

Nothing worse than an idiot with a valid point

"Uh-oh!" - the first person to throw a boomerang.

do army ants volunteer or do they have a draft

Never trust a shark that calls you "chum."

My GF told me to whisper "sweet nothings" in her ear. I whisper to her "my bank account number" because that has nothing in it...

If there was a movie about my "Entourage" it would just be me walking around with Ben and Jerry's in my hand

My insecurities do not define me... I am not the definition of my insecurity. Why, what did you hear?

This summer I'm sending a less fortunate child to John Cougar Mellen Camp.

I want someone to teach me how to write a self-help book.

On a scale from 1 - animal cruelty ... how bad is it if I give my dog Listerine strips?

In baseball the term "going yard" means hitting a homerun. Here in Biloxi it just means peeing outside

If I ever kill this mosquito I'm going to dismember him and mail him in tiny bug pieces home to his family

I just realized that I will probably never sleep in a heated water bed again.

I tried to throw that leftover cake in the trash but I missed and hit my mouth

I used to think my GF was into some kinky stuff when she kept police, nurse and maid uniforms in her closet… Turns out she can't hold a job.

With the NSA shutting down its illegal surveillance of us, it's like we're all losing a Big Brother.

I would totally be a UFC fighter if I wasn't as ticklish as I am...and fat

Thats an outright lie because your pants are clearly on fire, sir.

Dick Burns is my favorite person's name that sounds like an STD symptom.

If you want to work at IKEA you've got to learn to love your shelf.

I'm going to incorrectly correct people today. Then I'm going to sincerely argue my point.

You're telling me a door sang "Light My Fire?"

But, why would I want to iron my waffles?

Maybe the son of God's first name was meant to be Cheeses.

You know, there's just not enough frolicking in the world.

I finally decided to divorce 3 of my wives. I thought it was very bigamy.

I gave away smiles all day. Not one was returned. Awesome. My gift was worth keeping.

New research finds that frequent use of a selfie stick will result in selfie-elbow and will therefore impede the ability to pleasure yourself.

So what you are saying is that you're a Bisexual Hermaphrodite? How the hell does that work?

Sometimes I lie awake at night, sleeping.

Cops aren't racist, they're just blacktose intolerant

If a post has zero likes, Facebook should make it say "Nobody likes this"

A virus that sleeps around is called a fluzie.

I blame myself for blaming everything on myself.

Sure, I feel good after I exercise? But you know what makes me feel just as good in less time? Ice Cream.

I think when you match with someone on Grindr it should say "You've got male!"

I spend all my money on bar food. Pretty soon I'll be a jalapeno pauper.

"Did you hear a swarm of bees were arrested?" "They were caught in a sting operation"

Just wondering if vampires get cavities.

"If you're happy and you know it" stop posting it on Facebook because some of us like living depressing lives

The enemy of the blood orange is the crip orange.

New relationship: holds fart until they leave the room. Old relationship: holds fart until they enter the room.

Before we talk about this very complicated topic, you should probably know that I read several sentences about it in an article once.

Dr. Oz came to the aid of 2 people in a car crash on the NJ Turnpike, making this the first documented case of Dr. Oz helping anyone.

Kanye West's honorary degree makes him the highest educated person in the Kardashian family.

Just robbed a shepherd but my getaway car broke down so now I'm on the lamb.

It's not stalking if they don't see you

A 94-year-old man graduated from college after starting 75 years ago. His next plan is to move back in with his parents.

I think my "Beach Body" drowned and died a long time ago

I'm waiting for "granddad bod" to become popular because that's where my breasts are currently at

I want to write a book about procrastination but I've been putting it off

I went to the gym today...well actually I just drove past the gym today...well actually I just Googled "gym" and then I got tired

You don't have to tell me you're depressed. Your Members Only jacket says it for you.

DAD: What did you get your Mother for Mother's day?
JAKE: I accepted her Facebook friend request.

It would appear Daenerys Targaryen has seen 'How To Train Your Dragon'

I'm not worried about my kids seeing my search history because I end all my searches with "asking for a friend.

Funny, I don't remember having amnesia.

Just saw a goth kid smoking an e-cigarette. Vape-ire?

A bigger Brady football scandal was that time Marsha got hit in the nose the day before prom. This is just stupid.

A fun thing to do on a quiet Saturday is to go to a playground and when someone asks which kid is yours tell them you haven't decided yet.

Why I'm Not Working Out Today? Because extra fries sounds better than exercise

Just now found out that Stephen Hawking is British, which is somewhat mind-blowing because I never even noticed an accent.

Pretty excited, just found out my gym changed my status from "member" to "esteemed donor".

My only fitness goal is to look good enough that if I ever posed naked people wouldn't see it and say, "Wow, that's so brave of him!"

I wanna put out a magazine for the bisexual community called Biweekly. It comes out weekly. Or biweekly. IDK, guess I can't have it both ways.

Eventually I'll go on a diet, but right now I'm working really hard on perfecting my "before" picture.

American Idol announces its last season. Asked his reaction, Taylor Hicks says "Sir can you spare any change, I'm cold & hungry."

Matt Bacak I'm undefeated as a boxer because I've never boxed.

My superpower is indecisiveness, I think.

Happy Moulter's Day to all my bird and reptile friends.

I really want my children to have all the things I couldn't afford. Then I want to move in with them.

Test-tube babies should feel free to celebrate Mother's Day by sprucing up their old Petri dishes with fresh flowers.

Many people don't know this, but The Smurfs are based on a true story.

The founder of Weight Watchers has died, thus proving that dieting doesn't help.

I once held up a bank but had to put it down when my arms got tired.

♫ Heard it from a friend who Heard it from a friend who Heard it from another you been Doing a podcast ♫

Weight loss surgeons, live off the fat of the land.

I Can't Believe It's Not Butterface

Sending the wrong message sends the wrong message to those who receive messages.

"I like big tubs and I cannot lie!" - Sir Bathes-A-Lot.

Sorry I missed your call. I was busy counting how many rings it would take until it went to voicemail

You are never too old, to be too old.

When on holiday in Las Vegas, you're drunk and you happen to pick up a hooker... Check to be sure it's not a tranny or you'll get shafted.

How can women take boiling hot wax, pour it all over their private area, rip the hair out by the root and still be afraid of spiders?

Dad: I created your life and I can ended just as quick!
Jake: Yea I know, mom said 15 seconds.

I come from a long line of conga dancers.

No one really learns how to be a shoplifter... They pick it up as they go along.

I knew dinner last night was not going to go well when I overhear the waiter talking about the 'Five Second Rule'.

Congratulations to Princess Charlotte Elizabeth Diana on earning an extra name for being superior to the paltry proletariat.

Floyd Mayweather said he's willing to fight Manny Pacquiao again. Fight fans responded, "WE'RE GOOD."

Expect a HUGE birthday gift, Son! I hit it big thanks to a lucky email from Nigeria. I'm going to Western Union to make it all happen!

The 1st step to overcoming compulsive lying is to complete 40000 pushups everyday like I do

"Hey, what should we call this hole in the ground where we're getting our drinking water?" "Well, ...

Doctor, these pain pills you prescribed me aren't working. I feel no pain at all!

Imagine God has like a Tinder thing in heaven and once you die he either swipes right or swipes left

You know what doesn't go well with wine? Amazon prime one click shopping!

Nothing more dangerous than running with scissors, right? What about the guy chasing you with a rock?

McDonald's had produced a commercial using the song: "Head, shoulders, knees and toes" It's the most honest ad about burger ingredients.

(The following posts took place between November and December 2015. These events did not happen in real time)

January 2015

"Every time I eat a club sandwich my mouth bleeds." Did u take out the toothpicks? "Duh. Yeah. I ate those first."

I'm only stripping to pay for my Netflix subscription.

I like to combine Saint Patrick's Day with Cinco de Mayo. So I drink too much and hand out fake green cards
Today is Cinco de Mayo, where we have a fence to keep Mexicans out but celebrate and exploit their culture.

For Cinco de Mayo, I went to an authentic Mexican restaurant. The waiter poured me a glass of water and advised me not to drink it.

FUN FACT: Han Solo's real name is Hanford Solonkowski. He plays the accordion, writes poetry, & just loves stories about unicorns.

Saying "May the 4th be with you" makes you sound like a nerd with a speech impediment.

Of course I'm excited. Didn't you see the three exclamation points I added to the end of my reply?

I pissed off Star Wars fans today by telling them to live long and prosper.

Luke never married because a long long time ago there wasn't enough therapy to help him cope with kissing his sister

Here's a Star Wars fun fact. Never knowing his father, and having lost his mother, Anakin Skywalker was the inspiration for Little Orphan Ani.

Bill Clinton will be the first ever, "First Man" Bill says he likes the title, and will add it to his online dating profile

I'm worth It because I don't cost that much to begin with!

I'm going to have 'free wifi' engraved on my tombstone to ensure my family visit me when I die.

I know it's time to do laundry when the only clean pair of underwear I have left say, "spank me

If the royal baby had a sex change it would be the baby formally known as Prince.

The secret of a long marriage? Have a date night once a week with fine wine and candle lit dinners. She goes on Tuesdays, You go Thursdays.

I went for a jog this morning and it reminded me why I decided to get fat
Uncle Sam won fight. Mayweather would owe about $48 million in taxes, Pacquiao will have to fork over $32 million.

In my neighborhood, there is a sign said "drive like your kids live here" so I sped up and got the hell out of that neighborhood.

The Baltimore mother who went viral smacking her idiot son has 147 job offers to beat the hell out of other idiot kids

I want to be a modern pirate. I shall buy an iPatch !!!!!

Marco Polo is the first Netflix Original Series to take place entirely in a swimming pool.

The greatest thing about working hard is knowing that your tax dollars will be well spent.

Kate Middleton gives birth to a I DON'T GIVE A SHIT, THIS IS AMERICA....

I have the reflexes of a cat. Unfortunately the cat is Garfield.

I still give my lunch money to the person who bullied me in high-school. He works the counter at In and Out. lol

I bought my GF a star. She said she'd rather have some space. There's no pleasing that woman

A new study says 1 in 3 Americans could have diabetes by 2050. Forget gold. Invest in insulin

How come people who "tell it like it is" always forget to mention that they're assholes?

Alcoholic man with no legs has had no luck with 12 step programs. Shocking Statistic 82% of the people killed by lightning are male. Women appear to be better grounded.

Comedy routine March 2016 Mizos Juke Joint, Ocean Springs, Mississippi....

As seen on YouTube. ☺

Thank you very much. I'm a little nervous. Coming up on stages. Scary..

They say you'll never get over your fears unless you conquer it. When I was a kid, I was afraid of heights. Now, I'm high all the time.

I was in in the restroom at the and I was barely sitting down when I heard a voice in the other stall: "Hi, how are you?" Rich: (embarrassed) "Doin' fine!" Next Stall: "So what are you up to?" Rich: "Uhhh, I'm like you, just sitting here." Next Stall: "Can I come over?" Rich: "No, I'm a little busy right now!!" Next Stall: "Listen, I'll have to call you back. There's an idiot in the other stall who keeps answering all my questions!

I just recently sent a hallmark card to one of my neighbors. :

My tire was thumping.
I thought it was flat.
When I looked at the tire...
I noticed your cat. Sorry!
+
So your daughter's a hooker,
and it spoiled your day...
Look at the bright side,
she's a really good lay.

I used to be a butcher, but I got fired. One day I backed into the meat grinder and got a little behind in my work.
I was working in an orange juice factory, but I couldn't concentrate.

I once worked at Pepsi, I got fired their to. Tested positive for coke.

Just robbed a shepherd but my getaway car broke down so now I'm on the lamb.

Old yes I'm old. When I was a kid, the dead sea was just sick.
When I was in 1st grade, we didn't have history.
I knew Burger King while he was still a prince.

You're so old, an "all-nighter" means not getting up to pee.

I still got it though….

You heard of the mile high club….Why last week I flew back from Sand Diego and I joined the half mile club….I was by myself.

The stewardess was so old she was telling another stewardess about a three some with the wright brothers..

And FAT ooh She was so fat the plane hit a little turbulence and she sat on an iPhone and turned it into an iPad.

She wore a pair of high heels and struck oil.

My ex-wife and I never had good sex, heck we never had sex.sex.
We get undressed and couldn't stop laughing….

It's a little tougher at my age. I could take some Viagra but that's like putting a flagpole on a condemned building

My ex-wife would call me up at work calls me up gets me all hot and tells me to come over there's nobody home, I get over here nobodys home….

Just recently divorced all of my wives I know that was bigamy

"Mr. Wilens, I have reviewed this case very carefully," the divorce court judge said, "and I've decided to give your wife $5275 a month." "That's very fair, your honor," says Rich. "And every now and then I'll try to send her a few bucks myself."

I have a maroon friend...no coffee just 5 wives.

Do you know why Mormon women don't have any kids over 35? Because 36 is too many..

Kids. I have grandkids your age. Running around the pool at the hotel. Lady comes up to me and asks. Is your grandson Sam? Yes lady why? Well he is going pee pee in the pool.
I said look lady, boys will be boys.
She said yes, but it looks kind of funny, he's on the diving board....

I just smoked a bowl of some of my "medicinal pot". It's so good my spell check is even like "dude what are you saying?"

My Rodney: I fixed my pot problem. I joined AA. Well. MA AA for pothead...I did it for my PO... I still smoke, I just go under a different name.

Its better for me than beig a workaholic. When someone mentions work, I start drinking.

I bought my KID, son Jake a bow and arrow for his birthday. He bought me a jacket with a bullseye on the back

GEORGE CARLIN: Hi Gang. 7 words. Scott Lame, AL sleet

Im a catch.... I have a job, house car and good credit... Hundreds in the bank..

I don't have much going for me but I am Rich..., No seriously I was filthy Rich but then I took a shower. Then the cops found out and made me give it back...

How long you been married. 10 years. I was with the same woman for ten years, then my wife found out.

Love Vegas. Love it here// I play a lot of poker. My GF cheats at poker. She puts her arm under the table and gives me a wink and her hand beats me every time.

She lifted up her blouse and I was left holding a pair

She would bring her niece for luck. I'd flirt with the niece but still wound up upping the ante

One night I won every hand and still ended up in the hole.

What stays in Vegas, ya right....Here's what just happened to me......
I saw a gas station in here in Las Vegas with a HUGE sign saying "Free Sex with Fill-up."

Not to be confused with Alabama... Soon a local redneck pulled in, filled his tank and asked for his Free Sex.

The owner told him to pick a number from 1 to 10. If he guessed correctly he would get his Free Sex.

The redneck guessed 8, and the proprietor said; "Wow! You were close! The number was 7. Sorry. No sex this time." "I think that game is RIGGED, and he doesn't really give away Free Sex."

Bubba replied; "No it ain't, Billy Ray. It ain't rigged. My WIFE Won Twice Last Week."

I pulled in, filled my tank, and then asked for my free sex. The blonde attendant gave me a ticket for the free sex and told me to go down the hall and through the door. I was so excited I couldn't believe it. I walked down the hall and thru the door and there was this Bouncer type guy standing there with a handful of tickets. I said are you the ticket taker... He says No, I'm Phillip.....

About the Author

This is part of the bucket (pronounced Bouquet like Hyacinth) list is to write a book and perform the stand-up live. I did it.

It took 40 years but I returned to the stage. I always wanted to do comedy and I finally got my chance.

My show business career spans across the world playing such parts as Nathan Detroit in Guys and Dolls, The singing Russian and the beggar in Fiddler on the Roof , Gypsy, Anything Goes, Fiorello and many other musicals.

Doing stand up in the late 70's early 90"s came to an end because some people have to grow up. I grew up and had to make a real living.

It's now 2016 and I finished my third joke book and performed at the local comedy club.

Cross that off the list.

More
Books
From

PERFECT
PUBLISHING

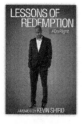    

    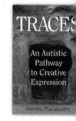

Your

Book

Here

www.PerfectPublishing.com